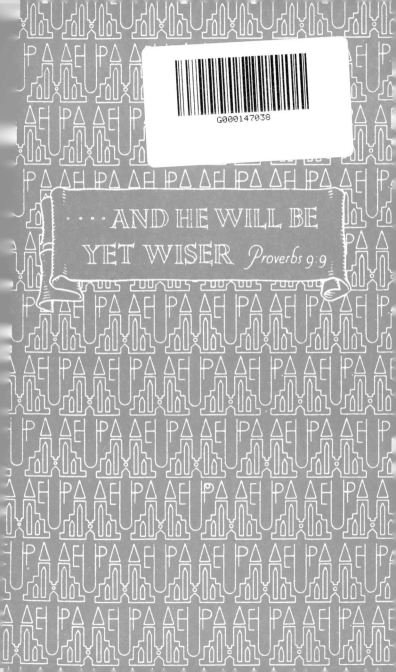

··· AND HE WILL BE
YET WISER *Proverbs 9:9*

"people with a PURPOSE"

A nostalgic journey through our British obsession
with self-improvement

Trevor Barnes

FOREWORD
BY PETER SNOW CBE

This book celebrates a publishing legend. About twenty years ago I stood in front of a display of all those familiar black and yellow books and wondered how soon they would run out of titles. That was when Teach Yourself had been going for fifty years. Today, after seventy years and more than 500 books, that tireless pursuit of readers hungry for knowledge shows no sign of flagging. In this enchanting anthology, Trevor Barnes savours the variety and eccentricity of subjects from *Teach Yourself Chinese* to *Teach Yourself Candlemaking*. He invites us to enjoy some of the quainter language and pokes fun mercilessly at the occasional pomposity. But, more than anything, this book is a revealing commentary on the changing needs of readers who want to learn and the shifting attitudes of those who would teach us.

Peter Snow

For UK order enquiries: please contact Bookpoint Ltd, 130 Milton Park, Abingdon, Oxon OX14 4SB. Telephone: +44 (0) 1235 827720. Fax: +44 (0) 1235 400454. Lines are open 09.00–17.00, Monday to Saturday, with a 24-hour message answering service. Details about our titles and how to order are available at www.teachyourself.co.uk

Long renowned as the authoritative source for self-guided learning – with more than 50 million copies sold worldwide – the **teach yourself** series includes over 500 titles in the fields of languages, crafts, hobbies, business, computing and education.

British Library Cataloguing in Publication Data: a catalogue record for this title is available from the British Library.

First published in UK 2008 by Hodder Education, part of Hachette Livre UK, 338 Euston Road, London, NW1 3BH.

This edition published 2008.

The **teach yourself** name is a registered trade mark of Hodder Headline.

Front cover copyright © Keystone/Getty Images
Copyright © 2008 Trevor Barnes

Typeset by Transet Limited, Coventry, England.
Printed in Great Britain for Hodder Education, an Hachette Livre UK Company, 338 Euston Road, London NW1 3BH, by Gutenberg Press Ltd, Malta.

Hachette Livre UK's policy is to use papers that are natural, renewable and recyclable products and made from wood grown in sustainable forests. The logging and manufacturing processes are expected to conform to the environmental regulations of the country of origin.

Impression number   10 9 8 7 6 5 4 3 2 1
Year   2012 2011 2010 2009 2008

ABOUT THE AUTHOR,
TREVOR BARNES

Trevor Barnes is a journalist and author. He is an award-winning reporter for BBC Radio 4 and, in a career spanning over twenty years, has worked extensively within its religious and current affairs departments. For many years he anchored Radio 4's *Sunday* programme and its sister programme on BBC World Service, *Reporting Religion*. He is a skilled documentary maker and has worked in BBC and commercial radio as well as BBC television. He also writes features for national newspapers.

Educated at the University of Oxford where he studied modern languages, Trevor is the author of eleven books, including two bestsellers and three ghostwritten autobiographies. He is also the author of three books for children.

To watch Trevor talking about this book, go to www.meettheauthor.co.uk and search for 'Trevor Barnes'.

CONTENTS

	PAGE
INTRODUCTION	1
I. IN THE BEGINNING – 1938 . . .	6
Salad days	7
A doctor writes	13
Flights of fancy	17
The King's English	26
Brain food	32
Nimble fingers	34
Rus in urbe	38
Three cheers	46
Current affairs	49
A country at war	59
Mind your language	65
A kaleidoscope of titles . . .	68
Post-war thinking	76
The tunnel's end	79
II. SUNLIT UPLANDS – 1940s . . .	82
The nobility of toil	86
Don't mention the war . . .	105
III. WORK, REST AND PLAY – 1950s . .	112
Employment exchange . . .	114
Sex and straight talking . . .	130
Happy families	138
Cultivating self-enlightenment . .	154
Back to the mainstream . . .	158

Television facts, figures and fables . . 161
"Up, up and away…" 164
Green and pleasant land . . . 173
Doing it by the book 178
Idle hours 186
Outdoor pursuits 197
Indoor fun 214
Teach Yourself at twenty . . . 222

IV. MODERN TIMES – 1960s . . . **227**

"People with a purpose" . . . 228
Hearth and home 230
R & R 241
Your eyes are getting heavy . . . 247

V. THE SAMOANS HAVE A WORD FOR IT . **250**

Spongebag in hand 250
Attend and persevere 261
Further afield 269
People on the move 276

VI. NEW WORLDS TO CONQUER – 1970s AND BEYOND **282**

All kinds of everything 282
The office 287
Getting on 290
Time off 292
Nouvelle cuisine 296
Roland Rat and the post-industrial age . 299
Make love not war 303

INTRODUCTION

Sometime in the mid 1920s the human race experienced a paradigm shift in its understanding of the world and its possibilities. With the slow inexorability of two tectonic plates colliding beneath the Earth's crust, human ingenuity and market forces converged to produce the frozen pea.

Thanks to one small step by the Brooklyn-born biologist Clarence Birdseye – a man who was to frozen foods what Einstein was to theoretical physics – food technology experienced a giant leap. The machinery was soon in place to freeze (and later distribute) vegetables for domestic consumption, and from 1934 the frozen food industry came into being. Where America led, Britain was soon to follow. So it was that shortly thereafter in 1938 the newly formed Birds Eye Corporation, swift to see untold possibilities in the UK, unveiled the prospect of frozen veg to a grateful British public.

That same year, the inaugural year of the Teach Yourself series, Evelyne White wrote her highly popular *Teach Yourself to Cook* and launched it on a nation soon to be suffering the privations of war.

Was this mere coincidence or were her publishers in tune with the Zeitgeist? Had they perhaps sensed the implications, mysterious and invisible as the link that binds the acorn to the oak, of this culinary revolution? And, if so, to what other popular movements and incipient fashions were they similarly attuned? To what other skills, trades, disciplines, and crafts might a needy British public be gently but authoritatively introduced?

Within the cauldron of such interrogatives the Teach Yourself phenomenon was born. Well, up to a point.

As Mrs White set to describing the best form of kitchen decoration ("a dado of glazed white tiles" with curtains of "squared gingham or the gaily-coloured oilcloths now available") or explained the benefits of the refrigerator over one's preferably north or north-east facing larder ("preparation of sandwiches for picnics can be done the evening before, or at any time when the housewife has some spare time"), "housewives" up and down the land sat up and paid grateful attention.

Thrift and inventiveness were prized; waste and false economy were derided. While tirelessly promoting "adventuring in cookery" (the addition of finely chopped ham to a macaroni cheese, for example, or veal cutlets with boiled cucumber), the author also conjured up endless recipes involving the recycling of left-over meat, fish and poultry. The appeal was as broad as the approach was persuasive. The kitchen ("the housewife's workshop") was not only a place in which to invent and to dream, it was also the engine room of the home and a practical metaphor for domestic stability.

In a deliberate move to include households of every class and income bracket, the author happily sang the praises of meat fingers and powdered egg while simultaneously devoting space to elaborate stuffings for roast fowl and the best way to dress a lobster. And as she did so, a template for future Teach Yourself books began to emerge.

Companion volumes on subjects as various as children's tailoring, good manners, house repairs and mothercraft combined a seriousness of purpose with a lightness of touch and addressed the reader in a winning tone of affection and respect. With each new book an author would enter into a tutorial relationship with the reader, gently but persistently encouraging him or her to form a confederacy of enthusiasm based on knowledge, learning and the slow accumulation of wisdom and insight.

Chronologically, 1938 is not so very long ago in the modern history of the country, but in fashions, language and attitudes it is a world – a planet – away. Abroad, the release of the film *Snow White and the Seven Dwarfs* was marked by massive popular acclaim (the German occupation and

annexation of Austria admittedly less so), while in
Britain the *Mallard* clocked a world speed record
for a steam locomotive of 126 mph and the
modern world marvelled. That modern world is
ancient history now but its social and cultural
evolution has been unwittingly tracked by a
landmark in British publishing, the Teach Yourself
series. Its individual volumes, like pictures in a
children's flicker book, tell of an ordered world
forever fixed in time. When read collectively and at
speed, however, they provide a continuous and
ever-changing narrative of pre- and post-war
Britain.

And that is what this book is about; part record
of Britain's changing and sometimes irrevocably
changed social landscape, and part "fancy-that"
compendium of the quirky, the unlikely and the
downright daft.

Along the way you will read how *Teach
Yourself Sex; Its Meaning and Purpose* (1951) gave
way to *Teach Yourself Tantric Sex* (2001); how
women who were making covered buttons for
their sons' caps or daughters' bonnets (*Teach
Yourself Children's Tailoring*, 1960) learned to
reappraise the whole notion of "women's" work
(*Teach Yourself Women's Studies,* 1996); how the
proper care of crocodile shoes and a vicuna
overcoat can give you an existential insight into the
meaning of life (*Teach Yourself to Live*, 1955); and
how, in the current catalogue, *Teach Yourself
Great Sex* (2006) happily coexists with *Keeping a
Rabbit* (2007). Well, it would, wouldn't it?

In seventy years, readers have been taught bee-keeping and bricklaying, good milk-farming and public speaking, stamp-collecting and palmistry; they have been taught how to write poetry and erotic fiction, fantasy and romance; they have been introduced to Chinese astrology, encouraged to act, taught how to relax, advised how to choose a pension, and persuaded to set up a small business; they have studied statesmanship from Pericles to Abraham Lincoln, history from the Sun King to Joseph Stalin, and mastered trades from welding to wiring.

In their free time, readers of the Teach Yourself series have been introduced to the pleasures of caravanning and lawn tennis, chess and calligraphy; in their working lives they have been schooled in performance appraisals and 100 ways to make money. And how they have been encouraged to communicate! In Slovene and Samoan, in Gujarati and Sanskrit, in Swedish and Gaelic. It's all been going on for seventy years and shows no signs of slowing down. What it will all look like in another seven decades' time, who knows? But here's hoping a fair few of you are around to find out.

Meanwhile, sit back as the house lights dim and the moving picture show flickers into life.

CHAPTER I

IN THE BEGINNING

1938

Brilliant ideas are often the simplest. This is fine by most of us because it saves a lot of effort. It also provides an excuse, if we haven't so far had a brainwave, to play down the smart alec who has. On one workaday Monday morning in the September of 1937, a senior member of the Hodder & Stoughton publishing team, one Leonard Cutts, had just such a brainwave and with it went on to make publishing history.

Hodder & Stoughton's top brass had assembled to ponder on how to give their newly formed imprint, The English Universities Press, the creative and financial boost needed to propel it into orbit. An educational series was proposed, to be based (every expense spared) on a pre-existing catalogue known as the "Self-Educator" series, volumes of which were collecting dust in the basement.

The books were brought up and passed around to the general approval of those present. The content was judged pretty sound, although the format left something to be desired. If the original titles were updated, given an eye-catching cover, and marketed under a snappy new title, they could be in business. But what was that title to be? Hmm. Puzzled glances were exchanged.

After a reverential silence during which chins were sagely stroked and the company's elder statesmen ventured every possible permutation of the unsuitable and the half-baked, inspiration struck. It chose as its conduit the young Leonard Cutts who, by the agency of the same mysterious alchemy that would later transform the Pluto Platter into the Frisbee and the Belly-go-Round (aka the Extruded Plastic Dingus) into the Hula Hoop, suggested "Teach Yourself". Bingo. Sherries all round and the cue for an early lunch.

SALAD DAYS

The next step was to get Evelyne White on board to teach the nation how to cook. She begins with a mild rebuke:

> Good cooking requires both time and effort,
> and many of our housewives are apparently
> unable or unwilling to give either to this all-
> important work.

But this is quickly followed by encouragement and
the reassurance that, with proper study, everyone
can serve up simple delicacies to equal those "of
France and other continental countries":

> This book has been planned so that the least
> culinary-minded housewife can produce food
> which is well cooked and appetising, and thus
> obtain such a knowledge of the art of cooking
> that she is spared much worry, and, may be,
> her family and herself a good deal of
> indigestion.

So, down to business and to a methodical survey of
kitchen equipment including that newest of new-
fangled devices, the refrigerator. To many it would
have been as mysterious as a magician's cabinet so
it needed basic explanation:

> This enables the housekeeper to keep
> perishable foodstuffs in perfect condition, and
> allows of salads and cold foods to be served
> quite cold.

With her talk of fish kettles, ramekin cases, and
soup ladles, White may occasionally transport you
to below stairs at "Gosford Park" but the appeal is
resolutely to the average (i.e. well off) household
with upwardly mobile aspirations and a store

cupboard of household necessities that include pearl barley, grated Parmesan cheese, gravy browning, meat jelly, rennet, sago, sardines, sultanas and tapioca. This was to be boosted, if possible, by anchovy essence, candied peel, chillies, French mustard, and horse-radish cream. Like a prototype Domestic Goddess, she took us seductively into her groaning larder to let us feast our eyes on provisions unimaginable – all of this a good seventy years before Nigella Lawson did the same on the telly but only two years before food rationing in Britain put paid to such plenty for the next fourteen years.

For a decade and more householders would recall sightings of bananas with the incredulity normally reserved for giant pandas mating successfully in captivity. General reaction to chillies, Parmesan, and French mustard in a neighbour's store cupboard, therefore, can only be guessed at.

Praise for *Teach Yourself to Cook*

It is no coincidence that the palm for culture and for cooking is by general consent awarded to the same race. To be a good cook is certainly one of the most useful of all achievements, and Mrs White has provided a most practical manual in a small compass.

But *Teach Yourself to Cook* was no mere recipe book. It was part of a series which, from the outset, was designed to embody the highest ideals and intentions. As the series editors noted in a postscript to the first edition: "*Teach Yourself to Cook* will add as much to the cultural development of the woman graduate with first-class honours as will *Teach Yourself Good English* to the clever engineer who is tongue-tied when he is forced to explain himself to the laity."

The cleaning equipment no housewife should be without.

Bass Broom	Kitchen-aid with rubber handle
Scrubbing Brushes	Wash-leather
Carpet Sweeper	Long-handled Sweeping Broom
Short Soft Banister Brush	Wire Stove-brush
Dish-cloths	Metal Pan Scrubber
Sink Brush	Glass Cloths
Dish Mop	Pails (2 galvanised)
Sink Tidy	Oven Cloths
Dustpan	Plate Brush
Soap Dish	Pudding Cloths
Floor Mop	Roller Towels
Vacuum Cleaner	Tea Towels
House Flannels	
Washing-up Bowl	

Teach Yourself to Cook, 1938

As a book on cookery proved, prospective titles were not centred on academic subjects alone. Breadth and accessibility were central to the Teach Yourself worldview along with a commitment to learning in its widest possible sense. Or, as the editors themselves put it:

> These books ... are designed for use in living, not to enable you to decorate yourself with a little snobbish "learning". The test of your culture is the measure of your ability to tackle any situation that life presents, and though you know the names of all the stars and can recite *Hamlet* backwards, if you are helplessly defeated before a cut finger or the taps on the gas-stove you have very little claim to call yourself a cultured person.

Boldly declaring that "dull textbooks are dead", the editors also realised that the appearance of the books was of central importance in the task of attracting new readers. "Although they cost only two shillings each" they were to be "beautifully bound in blue cloth of the most attractive and modern design" so as to appeal to the widest possible cross-section of would-be students:

> All honour to our fathers who sucked their learning from those dreary-looking volumes which an earlier age seemed to think a necessary accompaniment of "instruction". All honour, but, let us say at once, no emulation!

By today's standards the initial list was cautious despite the high idealism of its stated intentions. *Teach Yourself French*, *Mathematics*, *Embroidery*, *Good English*, *Public Speaking*, and *Latin* may not exactly give the impression of being at the cutting edge of popular pedagogy but, in its day, the series was groundbreaking in its commitment to the democratisation of learning.

What was more, the sales reps responsible for giving the books the hard sell felt the series title definitely had legs and reported back that booksellers thought so too. The format was working like a dream and they were soon flogging books by the yard. Three cheers at head office and doubles all round.

Each subject was prized not only for its intrinsic worth but for its contribution to the greater whole. Each subject, whether a highbrow academic discipline or a tradesman's everyday skill, was valued equally as a vital piece in an ever-expanding jigsaw of knowledge and culture. Whether philosophy or practical concreting, chemistry or embroidery, mothercraft or algebra, all branches of learning were valued alike as intellectual and cultural pursuits the mastery of which made men and women fully human.

Teach Yourself Embroidery (1938), "the art of enriching a fabric by stitchery and one of the oldest of the arts", for example, sat unself-consciously beside Mathematics in the fledgling Teach Yourself catalogue not least because it was written by "perhaps the greatest living authority on this subject" (Mary Thomas). The guiding principle was learning for learning's sake; and, moreover, learning through the good offices of the most competent experts of the day.

> **Tips and Hints from *Teach Yourself Embroidery***
>
> *Almost any embroidery stitch can be used to work an initial or monogram. A cipher or monogram on a jumper or scarf adds much to its intrinsic value, and on household linen a good letter imparts an air of dignity to bedlinen, table napkins, mats, towels and so forth.*

A DOCTOR WRITES

That same year, another expert (for reasons of professional confidentiality, known only as "a wise family doctor") compiled *Teach Yourself The Household Doctor* as an invaluable household reference book on everyday medical matters.

You want to keep well. You want to keep your family well. But, if there is an illness, if there is an accident, you want to know what to do promptly and without fuss. Here is the book to help you. It is pleasantly written so that you can pick it up at odd moments and absorb its instruction. Then you will avert a great many crises and be ready for those that are bound to arrive.

Readers were reassured that, by concentrating on health first and sickness last, the book would avoid "the pitfall of gloom inseparable from unrelieved study of sickness". Knowing also that "the author has had experience of doctoring in many parts of the world, from tropical heat to Arctic cold" they could confidently put themselves in his more than capable hands. "Keep his advice in a handy place at home" was the editor's helpful suggestion at the outset.

Stress-busting the Household Doctor's way

The contented mind is a blessing which helps the body to be healthy. Anger, irritation, excitement, worry – all these must be subdued, for these emotions tell upon our health. Be temperate in all things – in food, in drink, in work, in worry – and as much as lieth in you, live peaceably with all men.

The good doctor explained the importance of diet and exercise, had special chapters on nursing mothers, "the middle years", and the care of the elderly and, in all things, addressed the reader in a homely but authoritative voice. In matters of prevention his advice was uncomplicated. Regular meals were essential, with breakfast at 8 a.m., dinner (or lunch) at noon, tea at 4.30 p.m. and supper (or dinner) at 7.30 p.m. Moderate exercise or "physical jerks" was recommended as was the regular evacuation of the bowels ("The establishment of an after-breakfast habit may easily be accomplished by those who will give the needed time and trouble to it").

Interestingly, too, the doctor stressed the importance of what style magazines these days call "detox diets", advising plenty of water to keep the kidneys working. He even had a separate section on the importance of psychological well-being which, although written in his distinctly antique way, prefigured the dangers of "stress" long before this had become a medical fad of the late twentieth and early twenty-first centuries. This is of particular importance to the man in his middle years. True, his physical needs must be addressed:

> Plenty of greens ... and other foods which contain roughage ... Less meat; no seasoned foods; little (or preferably no) alcoholic drink; tea in moderation; coffee is not so good. The daily evacuation is essential; if missed, then a saline aperient is good, though many take liquid paraffin more or less daily.

In those days, evidently, people knew what an aperient (saline or otherwise) was in the first place – just as they had a working grasp of the more unusual uses to which liquid paraffin could be put. But it is to the inner man that the doctor directs his greatest attention:

Cultivate a mind free from agitations. Loss of temper and the tendency to worry are both things which make us grow older. Therefore try to acquire the calm, untroubled mind which goes with health; and may it be your good fortune to be free from money worries, which are so often the bane of advancing years.

He stops short of explaining how this near Buddhist state of detachment is to be achieved in practice, however, and instead summarises his survey of middle age with a no-nonsense breeziness that is clearly meant to reassure:

Fresh air every day; windows open at night; plenty of sleep; and a contented mind – these are some of the things that lead on to a happy and wholesome old age.

No point blinding the reader with science. Next, please.

Another partial (i.e. total) evasion occurs when the doctor turns his mind to sex education and "the teens". This was the thirties, after all, and a good twenty-five years in advance of Philip Larkin's official start date for sexual intercourse. While admitting that "in the days of the last century" children were "put off with evasive or untrue answers", he offers very little in the way of practical suggestions as to how to remedy the oversight. After a cursory allusion to hens laying eggs, pet white mice and rabbits producing "their little ones", he is content to say of sex education (to which, incidentally, he has never once referred in so many words):

> This should not be spoken of as something shameful; but the growing boy or girl may be told quite simply and seriously by father or mother that "we do not talk about these things".

And, erm, that's it. On to the next topic – care of teeth in childhood. No, we shall have to wait thirteen more years for sexual enlightenment – until *Teach Yourself Sex; Its Meaning and Purpose* (1951) makes its tentative though much-needed appearance on the Teach Yourself list. It was worth the wait.

FLIGHTS OF FANCY

As British Prime Minister Neville Chamberlain fruitlessly shuttled back and forth between Britain and Germany with documents bearing meretricious reassurances of peace, the people held their breath and hoped vainly that war would indeed be spared them.

Squadron Leader Nigel Tangye of the Royal Air Force (RAF) was probably not one of the hopeful. As a serviceman himself he would, more than most, have realised the imminent threat of military action and his book *Teach Yourself to Fly* (1938) was probably published, if not written, with this uncomfortable possibility in mind. His introduction, however, gave none of this away.

We meet young Tangye four years before he has had the opportunity to be taken up in a plane at all. Even so he has begun to study every textbook on flying he can get his hands on and, after a few months' reading, has qualified as a pilot – in his mind's eye, at least. One evening he might take to the air in a single-seater fighter to enjoy "a glorious half-hour of aerobatics", the next day he might content himself with being second officer on a scheduled airliner. From time to time he would take a break from flying a conventional machine and take to the controls of a sea-plane, changing "its element from blue water to blue sky by opening up the throttle of its engines and coaxing it to rest on its wings, silver and shining in the sun". When he has his first real lesson, of course, his fantasy world nosedives into the tarmac immediately as his basic ignorance of the "movement of the rudder bar" becomes apparent.

The story is typical of the Teach Yourself approach of the time and represents an innovation in textbook thinking. The inclusion of a personal story of youthful innocence became a much-repeated stylistic device adopted by so many Teach Yourself authors that it is impossible not to conclude that this was actively encouraged as the preferred house style. It seems that engaged but unforced mateyness was the desired technique to get the average reader on side from page one. In short, the book was aimed at the general audience not the specialist, at the enthusiast not the academic, at the lively mind not the pedant. And it was a recipe that proved extremely popular.

But, for the moment, back to Squadron Leader Tangye who is quick to point out that "however confident the reader may feel when he has reached the last page, it will not be advisable for him to go to an aerodrome and jump into a waiting aeroplane in the belief that he will be able to fly it". Well, there's a relief. Even so we are transported back to a time in the late 1930s when even aircraft were comparatively rudimentary machines that inexperienced RAF pilots could be trained up on in double-quick time before they took to the skies to defend the country from attack.

In Tangye's day, there was a pared down simplicity to the basic flying machine which meant that ease of manoeuvre was pretty standard. A look at one figure in *Teach Yourself to Fly* (see Figure 1) suggests a decidedly no-frills type of arrangement and recalls the age of the first automobiles, which could be bought and driven in the same day without any practice or prior instruction.

Nostalgia for a lost era

Almost gone are those happy, carefree days when a new type of aeroplane would appear out of the sky and land on the aerodrome, and the owner would come over to you and say, "Like to try her?" There are, alas! too many gadgets about an aeroplane now for an owner to feel so confidently generous.

Teach Yourself to Fly, 1938

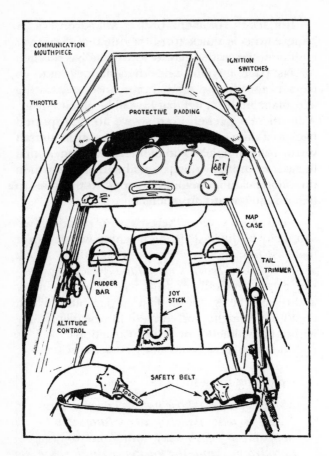

Figure 1 Interior of cockpit showing controls, dashboard and other fittings, *Teach Yourself to Fly*, 1938

Clearly *Teach Yourself to Fly* is a specialist book
directed not so much at the moneyed middle class
as at an extremely select and privileged substratum
of that class. Or so it appears. After a moment's
thought two other potential groups of reader come
to mind: first, the armchair aviator of every age;
and second, the young man who, though he may
not have known it then, would shortly find himself
on an airfield in the south of England being trained
to take to the air to fight for King and country in
the shortest time available. Indeed, the foreword
to subsequent editions spells this out:

> When this book was published it had a happy
> compliment paid to it. It was recommended by
> the Air Ministry to prospective R.A.F. pilots as a
> suitable book for their study. Since then we
> have passed from peace to war, but I have kept
> the flying instruction right up to date and the
> aircraft on which it is based is of the type
> extensively used in the Service for elementary
> instruction.

However, Tangye feels it necessary to apologise for
one or two references to the civil aviation scene
that are no longer available, adding – on a
touchingly elegiac note – that these "form a
sentimental reminder of a world of long ago". The
Squadron Leader's language, similarly, is of
another age:

> Incidentally, your instinct will often play you
> false when flying. Treat it as a fickle jade and
> you will do much better. When you are flying in

cloud by instruments, your instinct will often all but persuade you that your instrument is lying. The needle shows you to be flying straight, but your instinct shouts in your ear, louder and louder, that you are turning to the left. Be strong, and pay no attention to its voice.

Although by the third edition the country is well and truly at war, Tangye cannot bring himself to remove a passage clearly written in more peaceful times when the romance of flying was not dimmed by the realities of armed conflict. On cross-country flying, for example, he has this to say:

The exquisite joy of your first cross-country flight on your own can only compare with your first solo flight for ripe satisfaction. There is something about leaving the earth at one spot and coming down an hour later at another in a totally different environment without the gradual adjustment to one's senses that one experiences in a car that defies description. The most hard-boiled of men cannot fail to get a lilt when he feels his wheels touch for the first time on "foreign" soil.

PER ARDUA AD ASTRA

Where Tangye's approach comes into its own is in his winning blend of formal instructor and regular guy who has seen trouble and lived to tell the tale – an exciting one, to be sure, but not one told with excessive self-regard. It was the kind of understated bravado that played well to readers in those less showy times.

At one point he describes a potential disaster ("ugly metallic thumping noise ... engine stopped ... burst into flames ... cabin filled with smoke ... 600 feet up at 170 miles an hour ...") but uses it as a practical example of how to stay calm in a crisis and bring the plane safely to land. The key had been preparation:

> I am perfectly certain that I would have failed to pull off that landing had I not been in the habit of making every single landing on an aerodrome I had ever made in my career a make-believe forced landing. Take my tip, and do the same. Treat every landing as a forced landing, and triumph at the moment of trial is, believe me, worth all the trouble and patience of preparation for it.

It is in that "take my tip" that Tangye establishes himself paradoxically as both a man apart and one of the boys. A few pages later he cannot resist a chapter on aerobatics but, as usual, balances daredevilry with caution. "An airman's vanity," he knowingly opines, "is a most curious thing." And he goes on to describe how young men routinely feel the temptation to "aerobat" and show off to crowds of complete strangers looking up from the ground:

> Yet still that urge to stunt before them will be there – if he is young and gay and the world

feels good to him. But if he has reached the
flying age of discretion, he will resist the
impulse.

And here you get the distinct impression that while
Tangye has certainly reached the age of discretion,
he still retains a wistful admiration for the young,
gay pilot he was so many summers ago. In fact,
when he goes on to list the various stunts – from
loops, to stall turns, to flick rolls and half rolls and
slow rolls – appending a mere 500 words of
explanation to each, you feel he is really talking to
himself and his fellow daredevils who possess such
a level of flying competence already. The clear
subtext being: "Don't try this at home, sunshine."

Later editions of *Teach Yourself to Fly* carry a final
chapter "for you fellows in the Air Training Corps",
making it clear that the book will have practical
relevance for many a young man in times of war.
The reality is that many will be selected as air
gunners, wireless operators or air observers and
not as pilots. But by now they will have learned the
art of the stiff upper lip and acquired the ability to
meet success and disappointment with
equanimity.

   In its first year, *Teach Yourself to Fly* could
have been subsumed into an (albeit specialised)
sub-section of "Sports and Recreation" and gone
the same way as *Teach Yourself Motor Boating*. By
an accident of timing it did not. The book's back
cover was subsequently modified to puff later
editions as follows:

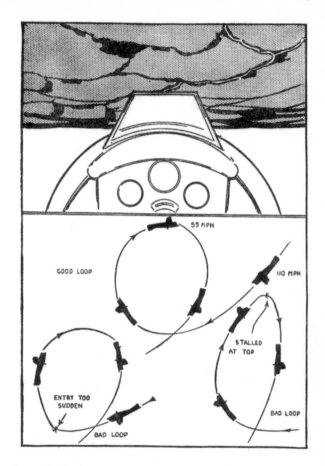

Figure 2 The loop, *Teach Yourself to Fly*, 1938

Your First Solo Flight

will be made a great deal sooner if you study this book, for you can master the theory before you even come into contact with the 'plane.

You can save your instructor's time and patience and that is

A SERVICE TO YOUR COUNTRY

This was far from an average volume for an average household. The timing ensured that *Teach Yourself to Fly* necessarily catered for an élite audience. As if to underline this, subsequent related and equally specialised volumes followed. *Teach Yourself Air Navigation* (1942) and *Teach Yourself Radio Communication* (1942) joined forces with books on Mechanics and Trigonometry as guides deemed "specially useful for members of the Royal Air Force and the Air Training Corps".

THE KING'S ENGLISH

Even in the circumstances of gathering national emergency in Britain, the civilian population and its civilised cultural values could not be ignored. In times of the gravest danger there was always scope to broaden the mind and look to the pleasures of peacetime that would surely follow an allied victory. And what better way to set the tone than with *Teach Yourself Good English* (1938). Subtitled "A practical book of self-instruction in English composition based on the work by G. H. Thornton, MA" it set out to examine the principles that underlie good written English, and to suggest the best ways in which the reader could achieve this:

> You may be learned in all the uses of restrictive and illative and copulative clauses, and yet be unable to compose a single sentence with lucidity and ease. The study of formal grammar is useful in itself, but it will no more help you to write than a knowledge of anatomy will help a lame man to walk. To have learned much and read much is of more value in learning to write good English than to have parsed and analysed half a library.

Classics scholars of a certain age and educational background may just about get the gist of this but most people under the age of fifty-something will gaze at Thornton's introduction as a monkey would a clock.

It is fantastic to credit that the 1938 edition was "completely revised and enlarged by Kathleen Baron, BA" as late as 1960 and still contained the following example of an albeit "badly" constructed piece of prose:

> "An old Oxford acquaintance of Hebrew extraction, who had adopted the name of an ancient Scotch family, tempted me (to invest unwisely in the stock market), and I fell. "For two years the dividends were paid. Yesterday the company went into liquidation and my few poor thousands have vanished into thin air like a ghost in Virgil."

And with the best will in the world, the would-be writer coming to English composition in the Age of Aquarius would have had a hard time getting by on "the essays of Addison, Hazlitt, Leigh Hunt, Macauley, R. L. Stevenson, Richard Jeffries, and W. H. Hudson" or even "contemporary writers such as Robert Lynd, E. V. Lucas, H. M. Tomlinson, Aldous Huxley, and Sir Arthur Quiller-Couch". "Contemporary" in 1960 clearly meant something different from "contemporary" in 1938 but the reviser seems not to have twigged and the difference was lost on her.

Yet G. H. Thornton's heart was in the right place even if Kathleen Baron's head was arguably somewhere else. After all, he was trying to persuade the amateur to read widely and to look for inspiration in every manifestation of the written word. Even, God forbid, in journalism:

> The ignorant tinker who wrote *The Pilgrim's Progress* wrote great prose because his ear was attuned to the language and cadence of the *English Bible*. Today the daily newspaper has taken its place. Instead of David's lament over Jonathan, we read of "Scenes in Stepney" or "Love Tragedy in Hyde Park". It would, of course, be foolish to condemn all newspaper-English as bad. In clearness and brevity you can learn much from the journalist; in the vivid presentment of facts his is a master hand.

But:

> If you wish to gain a good and flexible style,
> newspapers must not be your only reading, nor
> must you read them too much.

Nonetheless, the Teach Yourself series was not
above a bit of popularisation itself. And, thanks to
a smart idea on somebody's part, the book
established itself as something of a popular
milestone. Mr Thornton and his editors hit on a
brilliantly simple innovation which was to set the
Teach Yourself books apart from any other
competitor. They incorporated a series of exercises
in the second half of the book to be checked
against a corresponding series of specimen
answers contained at the back. Thus a reader
became a student and could test him or herself
against an objective standard. This was truly
groundbreaking, since not only were the books
approachable, accessible and friendly, they now
carried with them a hint of discipline and
compulsion. It was as if those readers who had had
no experience of 4th form English lessons at public
or grammar school were suddenly granted entry to
the classroom and could, metaphorically, sit side
by side with their more privileged fellow pupils.
With this book in their pocket they joined not only
a class but a veritable fellowship of semi-accredited
scholars. And Bob was, indeed, their uncle.

Men or women who had no education or only
rudimentary instruction as a child could make up
for this oversight by their own efforts as an adult.
Like Thomas Hardy's Jude they, too, could read

and better themselves but, *unlike* the tragic Jude, they could enjoy the luxury of guided tuition and make a stab at leaving obscurity behind. Exercise 15 in *Teach Yourself Good English*, for example, read:

> State which figure of speech each of the following exemplifies, and write out the meaning of each sentence in plain literal language:-
>
> 1. As a dog doesn't understand good English we naturally talk bad to him.
> 2. Some German words are so long they have a perspective.
> 3. Paris is not a city, but a Bedlam.

Day by day, month by month, the readers could work through exercises like these and know they were not working in a vacuum because their work could ultimately be "marked". Exercise 15 duly completed, they could turn to the "Key to Exercise 15" at the back of the book and see how their answers compared with the suggested answers printed.

> 1. Antithesis: This is a mild epigram which is literal enough as it stands.
> 2. Hyperbole: Some German words are extremely long.
> 3. Metaphor: The people of Paris go mad.

The device was not suitable for every title, of course, but where it was appropriate, it was included. In later volumes, the editors went to the trouble of including formal examination papers in the books and invited readers to complete them as they would a school or even university exam. The paper was then scrupulously marked and returned, graded, to each individual reader giving him or her the real impression of participating in actual student life. Each book became a personal tutor and the reader was left with the satisfaction of feeling part of a wider community of learning.

Moreover, the early volumes were written at a time when education was prized more than it is today and when self-improvement meant more than merely assessing your "emotional intelligence" or some such thing in the pages of a style magazine. Public libraries were not just places you nipped into to borrow DVDs; they were valued as real working engines of popular education – and even had books in them.

BRAIN FOOD

"He that will not reason is a bigot; he that cannot reason is a fool; and he that dares not reason is a slave." With the imperious words of Sir William Drummond, the English Universities Press prefaced its 1938 two shilling edition of *Teach Yourself to Think*, claiming grandly:

> There have been many books on the art of living, but not one quite like this. It has wit. It has humanity. It does not tell you how to become a millionaire, but a careful reading cannot fail to help you gain that mental mastery which is the true success.

Under chapter headings such as "Pride and Prejudice", "Propaganda and Rhetoric", "Sweeping Statements", "Potted Thinking", "Errors in Reasoning", "More Errors and Some Dishonest Tricks", the author of *Teach Yourself to Think*, R. W. Jepson, sought to bang the drum for logic and reason in private and public discourse. For logic, he believed, is "the cold douche that extinguishes the warm glow of sentiment".

Crikey. What next? A brisk rub down with *The Spectator*?

It is a strange book, this. Not so much an objective academic thesis, more an opinionated rant ... sorry, authored essay containing the collective personal insights of one individual. It was a shrewd marketing ploy since the readers could have their expectations of the gradually expanding series challenged and occasionally confounded. While one book would give them a sober, objective understanding of chemistry, say, or mathematics, or embroidery, another would provide them with a highly personal, left-field opinion that would more often than not startle and amuse. The series was big enough to incorporate these novelties, which had the added advantage of lending the whole endeavour a refreshing eclecticism – and the occasional surprise.

R. W. Jepson, for instance, was no academic philosopher but was allowed 154 pages to expound his own brand of wit and homespun wisdom. On the nature of superstition he writes:

> As someone aptly put it: "Scratch a stockbroker and you will find a savage!" Touching wood and carrying mascots are relics of the days of idolatry and magic. But are the days of magic and idolatry really gone? Do not many of us worship machinery, for example, just as fervently as our primitive ancestors worshipped sticks and stones? And then there is the man who will cheerfully send half-a-crown for a trial bottle of somebody or other's Vegetable Compound convinced that it will cure him of his aches and pains. He may be a sceptic in religion, but has he given up believing in miracles?

The book turns out to be largely based on a series of broadcast talks Jepson gave some time earlier and thus established him as a cultural commentator of the day, railing at what he saw as the iniquities of the age. The end result is little more than the "Why oh why" school of journalism in the middle-range popular dailies today, but it added a bit of unpredictability to a series of essentially sober titles.

In his conclusion, Jepson summarises his arguments and essentially reduces them to a couple of points; that language can be an obstacle to arriving at truth and that truth itself is only attained by logic and reason. Erm, yes, quite. While it would be difficult to disagree with such a generalised statement of the near obvious, understanding what precisely the book is "teaching" is open to question. The fourth edition (circa 1941) struggled to make things any clearer. And after a reworked introduction bemoaning the fact that "the second World War has brought its own crop of wishful thinkers and rumour-mongers", Jepson knocks out the old material verbatim. Can't improve on perfection, old boy.

NIMBLE FINGERS

Turning to the Teach Yourself list of 1939 it comes as a welcome relief to move from the cerebral to the practical and to Isabel Horner's *Teach Yourself Dressmaking*. With the country now at war and in belt-tightening mode, it seems likely that this volume was commissioned as a useful exercise in home economy. However, from the outset Ms Horner turns it into something else – a celebration of the simple delights of domestic life and a reminder of how life will be once again when the fighting is over. She begins with a tone of such breeziness that we would hardly know there was a war going on at all:

> "Some women dress – others merely wear a few clothes!" a witty old lady once remarked ...
> The art of dressing is well worth studying.

While many people will have found themselves preoccupied with the darker thoughts of war, Horner was determined to spread her brand of lightness and cheer. And who could blame her? The sheer uncomplicated ordinariness of her chosen leisure pursuit was a tonic in itself and one that the War Office would surely have approved of. After all, were not the simple pleasures of hearth and home part of the very fabric of the English way of life that these foreign aggressors were hell bent on trying to destroy? In this regard, Horner was surely as much a part of the Battle of Britain as our airmen would later prove in their Spitfires above the cornfields of southern England.

So to blazes with the war. Let's look to a future of gaiety and delight when women of every age and class can avail themselves of fabric in every colour and style to make this temporarily benighted country beautiful once again. Why, nowadays everyone can look smart and there's no excuse for drabness:

> Aids to attractive dressing are provided by magazines, newspapers, cinemas, theatres, and dress parades. Thanks to these, the provincial woman is now as well dressed as the Londoner.

Horner, as befits a Teach Yourself author, is the
great encourager. Not only will she encourage the
"provincial woman" to up her game, she will
cheerfully promote the art and craft of home
dressmaking so that everyone can have the
opportunity to explore her latent talents:

> Materials are so cheap, too, that a girl with a
> knowledge of dressmaking can quickly and at
> little cost, copy or adapt a style to meet her own
> needs. There are some lucky women who seem
> to have been born with a needle and scissors in
> their fingers! These can make, apparently as
> easily as a spider spins a web, a frock which
> simply cries out "Paris" to all observers. But
> less favoured ones need not despair ...

... of course not, because Isabel – if I may – is the
great inspirer, ready to jolly along the diffident,
cheer on the timid, and generally spread the
gospel of dressmaking far and wide. Come on,
girls, no excuse. Yes, some of you may be
naturals ...

> But less-favoured ones need not despair, for
> dressmaking is an art which can be learnt by
> anyone who will apply herself to it
> wholeheartedly.

Her approach is clear and logical. Starting with an
outline of the basic equipment, she progresses to
the minutiae of paper patterns and materials.
Thence to measuring, cutting out and fitting.
Everyday features such as sleeves, fastenings,

pockets, collars, and cuffs are explained in detail before she proceeds to give a master-class in such esoteric mysteries as circular flounces, godets, gathers, scallops, corded puffings, pipings, ruchings, shell edging, and braiding. The world of dressmaking was literally at her fingertips – and now it could be at yours for a mere two shillings and sixpence.

By the end of the book we have put all thoughts of war behind us. We are back in an ordered world of simple pleasures where hard work is rewarded and all can bring their hidden talents to glorious fruition.

Encouragement on the home front

It is strange that while the appellation "Home-made" is so highly esteemed when applied to cakes, jams, and other eatables, it is often a term of disparagement in connection with clothes. This, however, is not inevitable, and I can guarantee that any girl of average intelligence can, by diligent practice according to the directions given in this book, turn out creditable work which will transform the despised label of "Home-made" into an enviable one.

Teach Yourself Dressmaking, 1939

RUS IN URBE

Richard Sudell was a man plucked from the very same pod as Isabel Horner and he would do for the garden what Isabel had done for the wardrobe. *Make Yourself a Gardener* (1939) is another wartime book where mention of the war is non-existent – not because the authors or the editors wanted to brush it under the carpet but because they believed that the simple thoughts of peacetime were a natural and very human occupation in times of uncertainty and danger. Again one feels the War Office would have approved, citing books like this as the undeniable generators of national morale.

Make Yourself a Gardener begins, oddly enough, with a whinge:

> It is commonly asserted that all arts and crafts are gradually yielding to mechanisation and mass-production. The traveller packs a cine camera and some colour films instead of a sketch-book and palette. The lonely settler buys a radio set instead of a banjo, and his neighbours come over to listen, not to contribute to the evening's entertainment.

Disregarding the possibility that a neighbour with a banjo may be lonely for good reason, you get the idea. It is a regular refrain in many of the pre- and post-war Teach Yourself books that standards are slipping; that things are becoming that little bit more anonymous and impersonal with every passing year. *Make Yourself a Gardener* voices similar fears. Though with the best will in the world, it is still hard to fathom how the banjo was likely to improve things.

Mr Sudell, "one of the greatest living landscape gardeners, to whom many famous gardens owe their beauty", confidently asserts that "garden-making is almost the only non-mechanised hobby, almost the only one that cannot be ruined by competitive mass-production". Obviously he had never seen "Ground Force". Obviously. This was 1939, after all.

For Sudell, the gardener's world was a fraternity of equals where each met "on common ground, with a common purpose, and a common problem". It was a pursuit singularly free of snobbery, he claimed, (and you believe him) and one bound by an immutable law:

> A rhododendron takes as long to grow for a millionaire as for a cottager, a rose will bloom as freely in suburban gardens as in the rose acre of the castle grounds.

It was the garden as ultimate democracy.

The pages have an innocent feel to them, which is hardly surprising since they belong to a world that is so distant from ours; a world, for example, that has only lately come to terms with the "change in fashion that no longer regards open air meals as Bohemian". Even so, some of the author's preoccupations and considerations remain the same today:

I want to show the novice how to make the garden with a minimum of effort. In these days of speed and hustle, the average householder has but a limited number of hours to spend in his garden. The garden of to-day has to be fit to live in, and to look at, too; and it has to be made speedily.

Wait a minute, perhaps "Ground Force" got the idea from *him*, encouraging weekend gardeners to think like Louis XIV and bring a little of Versailles to Woking and Carshalton. Sudell certainly wants the reader to think big, as his chapter (and illustrations) on vistas and viewpoints bear out. The options he suggests for that "most thrilling moment" when you draw up your garden plan also indicate he has the larger garden in mind:

Do you expect your garden to provide the household with vegetables and fruit? Or is it to be merely an outdoor living room? Or just a picturesque setting for the house. Have you small children who need a part of the garden in which to play? Are there young people in the household who would like to play tennis or some other outdoor game?

The fact that he is considering a tennis court as a serious option clearly shows his sense of priorities. As befits a gardener "to whom many famous gardens owe their beauty" he has a tendency to think and plan on the grand scale, but he is careful to take the general reader with him. The general reader can, after all, dream.

Whatever income bracket he is aiming at, waste and excess are always frowned upon. Sudell's advice is to get the best equipment you can afford (which Teach Yourself authors, incidentally, would repeatedly tell you was as true for gardeners as it was for dressmakers, embroiderers, carpenters, bee-keepers, and motor-boat enthusiasts). Better to have little money and to treat one's few tools well, than to have all the money in the world and to neglect those tools simply because they can always be replaced.

Economy, tidiness and a dash of national stereotyping

Stainless steel is well worth its cost, though admittedly the cost is high at present. A wipe over with a wet rag, or a rinse beneath a tap, and the spade is like new, even after years of use. With the other type of spade, if the wet rag is followed by an oily rag before the spade is hung on its allotted peg in the tool-shed, its life will be long enough to satisfy even a Scotsman.

Make Yourself a Gardener, 1939

True, there was a war on, but reading the book today gives the distinct impression that England is slowly but inexorably moving into modernity. This is a world of increasingly affordable luxuries and of growing affluence for large swathes of the population. There will be privation and rationing to endure but you feel that not even enemy bombs will put accelerating living standards into reverse:

> The general style of modern architecture on the new housing estate today is good. There is not the slightest reason why you should not make an old-world garden in a plot attached to an ultra-modern sun-trap house, but there is every reason why this garden should not be prominent at first sight, so that the visitor is greeted by two conflicting styles.

Realistically (although the thought is left unspoken) the "new housing estate" with its "ultra-modern sun-trap house" is the domain of the relatively affluent middle class. It would have been highly unlikely for those living in the slums of the inner city to have pored over Sudell's sumptuous plans with the same expectations as their suburban counterparts. Box parterres, patios, and rose-strewn pergolas were pie in the sky if you lived in a tenement sharing an outside lavatory with three other families. And consequently the odd purple patch (of prose not broccoli) bears very little relation to "ordinary" people's lives:

> I can imagine an ultra-modern house, with an almost enclosed sun-trap garden behind it, surrounded by cement or hewn stone walls, from which there are perhaps several exits. And I imagine that beyond these exits the garden could assume an entirely different character, so that a keen gardener wishing to

turn this extra portion into an Elizabethan garden could do so without disharmony.

And, of course, anyone can dine at the Ritz.

While it is true that there is a distinctly middle-class bias to a book like this, there is a greater point to bear in mind. For one thing, social and economic opportunities were opening up to the masses. Slowly, perhaps; erratically, maybe. But the war would throw all society's cards in the air and post-war regeneration would reassemble them in an entirely different formation. Education and learning would become the agents of social change and self-instruction of the type the Teach Yourself books embody would ensure that knowledge was within the reach of all. Moreover, if the less well off could not afford the half a crown to buy the books themselves, they could go to libraries, colleges, night schools, and institutes to read them for free.

And, as always, people could dream. The sumptuous plans portrayed in the book (see Figure 3) are not just beyond the means of the average inner-city dweller, they would have been way beyond the reach of even the comparatively well-off suburban bank manager and businessman. Who but the landed gentry with staff to tend their gardens could have afforded a plot that included drive, garage, iris garden, pool, well, herbaceous borders, rose garden, herb garden, loggia, paved terrace, sundial, pergola, lawn, gravel paths and hard tennis court? Probably not even Mr Sudell. And certainly not slum dwellers planning their Elizabethan gardens or rose-strewn pergolas as they watched the sun set over the gas works. But in times of war there were probably far worse things to think of.

What is refreshing about the Teach Yourself approach to gardening (and the reason, one assumes, that people like Richard Sudell have always been chosen as Teach Yourself authors) is the friendly yet authoritative relationship that the author develops with the reader. When Sudell says "I believe in the good taste of the amateur gardener", you are left with the impression that he really means it.

When he goes on to say, understandingly, that "any shortcomings of the small garden are due to thin pocket books – rather than to inherent bad taste or ignorance" the reader feels once again that this eminent gardener is in sympathy with the everyday constraints on the ordinary amateur. Even so, Sudell will at times address the reader in a tone that suggests partly an eccentric schoolmaster rhapsodising over the finer points of some Latin verse and partly a Shakespearean ham playing to the gallery. On the uniqueness of the rose, for example:

> But whether he makes his rose garden an elaborate affair, or whether his roses are grown in a simple circular bed, he will have to consider them as a separate item in the garden lay-out. The reason for this is that Queen Rose is far too haughty a monarch to allow the common herd of garden plants to approach too closely. She demands a place in the sun, and a

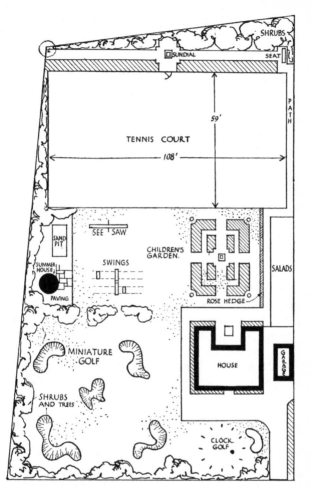

Figure 3 *Make Yourself a Gardener*, 1939

place that she is not asked to share with others. Only the lowest of dwarf attendants are tolerated in the rose beds.

For all the high-flown sentiments, however, and despite all the grand plans and the elaborate projects, the author is never a distant figure. A teacher, yes, but a teacher who is always on the student's side.

THREE CHEERS

Perhaps it was this unique approach of a friendly but authoritative author that caused the critics to sit up and take notice, commending the Teach Yourself books as something of a publishing phenomenon. A favourable review was published on the inside cover of *Teach Yourself Economics* (1939) and was duly accompanied by a bit of publishers' hype explaining the success of the enterprise.

> "An exciting new series," said *The Observer* when we launched the first of our "Teach Yourself" books. We have tried to keep it exciting – by which we mean that we have tried to make learning fun; we have tried to make our readers feel that these books are their friends. From the letters many of them have sent us we are encouraged to think we have not been unsuccessful.

Teach Yourself Economics set out to explain "its importance in the modern world, and stimulate an interest in the science that will lead to its true and proper appreciation".

Defining economics simply as "the study of man in his efforts to make a living", the author, chooses examples from the everyday with which the reader is familiar. "Consider the factory worker, the farmer, the shopkeeper, the doctor, the businessman etc. etc.", he writes, creating a model Trumpton wherein economics can be shown to operate in the familiar everyday world we know. His examples are very much of his day and have an antique quaintness barely recognisable in these less formal times. "Diminishing utility", for example, he explains as follows:

> Consider the position of a man in regard to suits of clothes. In this country, he must have one suit at least if he is to go out of doors at all. This suit will have considerable utility.

Had Evelyn lived to see shell suits, tracksuits, trainers and, God forbid, shorts worn by adults in public, he would have shaken his head in uncomprehending despair. Standards were rather different in his day:

> He may buy several suits and keep one for day time, one for evening wear, one for golf, one for motoring, one for gardening, and so on.

A suit for golf, for goodness sake? One for motoring and even one for gardening? Yes, indeedy, that was what it said. Those were the dress codes then – or at least for the middle and upper classes who alone could afford golf and a motor car in the first place. But we digress. There is an economic point to make:

> But the more suits he has of a particular kind (ie the more evening suits or the more golf suits), the less satisfaction does he get from an additional suit of that kind, until, if he keeps on buying such suits, there comes a time when he would get far more satisfaction by spending the money on something else.

The mind boggles at the prospect of anybody getting any satisfaction out of a golf suit, but no matter. There we have it; the principle of "diminishing utility" in a nutshell.

His section on "Equal Pay for Equal Work", however, is dated in a more fundamental way and it is worthwhile quoting Evelyn at length:

> There has long been agitation among women civil servants, for instance, that they should be paid at the same rate as men civil servants when they are doing exactly the same work, but the Government will not accept the principle. The problem bristles with difficulties, because it is not always easy to say what is equal work. Even where similar clerical work is being performed by a man and a woman, it is not certain that they are equally useful to the employer. The employer may have greater faith in the man's ability to cope with an emergency situation, or in his greater immunity from

illness, or in his greater ability to stand the strain of busy periods. Men will work under conditions that would be unsuitable for a woman, and they can be called upon to undertake jobs that an employer would hesitate to give to a woman.

Discuss.

Certainly the current edition of *Teach Yourself Economics* is free from such assumptions but both, in the end, are necessarily products of their time, using examples from contemporary life and giving the reader a taste of contemporary thinking.

CURRENT AFFAIRS

Among the many notable events of 1939 – the death of Sigmund Freud and the births of Tina Turner and Dusty Springfield – was the publication of the classic *Teach Yourself Household Electricity*, bringing people (to be truthful, women) face to face with the stark realities of the wartime economy:

If, in the days of peace, it was desirable to learn how to make the best use of electricity in the home, now, in the days of war, when fuel consumption is limited, it is imperative that *all* should understand how best to use electricity wisely.

"*All*", however, heavily italicised, was not strictly speaking to the target audience and, three paragraphs in, the game was up:

If reduction of consumption is now only hinted at instead of insisted upon, another housewifely duty has taken its place – to re-organize the uses to which electricity is put in the home.

Come again. "Housewifely"? Where did that spring from? "Housewifely duty"? Who said? Well, the clue to this double conundrum lay with the author, Caroline Haslett, CBE, who had been responsible for a related tome, *The Electrical Handbook for Women*, which begins:

The importance of electrical education is increasing daily, and especially so among women and girls who will in the future form the largest body of users of electricity for many divers purposes.

Well, not if one woman had her way they wouldn't. That woman, however, would take a few years yet to make her mark. The newly delivered Germaine Greer was that same year emerging into the electric light of a Melbourne maternity hospital and was destined to shape the future in a rather different way than Miss Haslett could then have guessed.

As yet in the dark over this pivotal Antipodean nativity, Haslett blithely asserted the primacy of women in the electrical front line of wartime economies. She began with a few facts to explain the general position: that the record annual consumption of electricity before 1914 in Britain was a third of that used in 1939; that the popularity of electrical goods was steadily increasing; and that their variety and ubiquity would continue to increase. But she didn't quite put it like that. Instead:

> It is but a short span in time since electric cookers and fires, vacuum cleaners and washing machines were timidly approached novelties, since electricity in the home meant electric light and little else; yet see to-day how far the well-electrified home outstrips these meagre limitations, how commonplace a sight is a well-equipped kitchen. We have accustomed ourselves quickly to television, and take for granted marvels the very inventors of which are still with us. To look far ahead is impossible, and we can be sure on only one point, which is that all domestic progress will take an electrically lit path.

As baby Germaine gnawed on a rusk planning her re-examination of woman's role in society, Haslett was busy expounding her own version of women's liberation:

> At one time the housewife who said, "I work in the house from morning till night", thought she exhibited a high degree of domestic virtue, but the woman who says this today stands self-condemned as a being lacking in imagination and backward in her ideas. Such a one, if she has not the initiative to acquire the modern technique and methods of dealing with her housework, deserves to work from morning till

night, but her attitude arouses exasperation rather than sympathy. To her one feels inclined to say, "Work in the house from morning till night? What a waste of a precious day! Do you really think that it was for that purpose that you were created with a heart, a brain, nimble fingers, active feet, normal intelligence, and a capacity for enjoyment? You poor house-bound woman! You'll be old for much longer than you're young; and when you are old, upon what will you look back? Years of housework from morning till night? Cannot you master, once and for all, this business of domesticity? Call on science to help you. Cease working like a horse and use horse-power. Learn to 'take the current when it serves', and give yourself time to LIVE – in short, what about an all-electric home? To-day this is no longer the privilege of the wealthy, but the possession of the majority. The easily-run electric home enables housewives to develop their personalities in their leisure hours, and the intellectual woman need not have a neglected home nor the domesticated woman a narrow life."

Phew. Not since *A Tale of Two Cities* has the world been subjected to so rousing an exordium. Could the Electrical Association for Women, formed fifteen years earlier "with the object of satisfying the electrical needs of women", have had a better figurehead than Caroline Haslett, CBE? It seems hardly likely. And she goes on to list some of the Association's achievements, chief of which was the promotion of understanding:

> ... understanding of the best use of apparatus, understanding of the care of appliances, understanding of elementary technical points, and a deep enough understanding of the problems of electricity distribution to appreciate the need for co-operation between supplier and consumer.

And, of course, the tacit understanding that if there was a vacuum cleaner in the house it would have been the "housewife" who was expected to use it, and, should the man of the house have wanted his golf suit pressing or the creases of his cravat smoothed out, it would have been his good lady wife who would have reached for the electric iron and the tie-press and duly obliged.

No doubt about it, Ms Haslett was a champion for her times. Unclouded by doubt or vacillation, her fidelity to the cause was absolute. And acolytes aplenty were lining up behind her to carry the torch (batteries most definitely included):

> Gradually, in the last fifteen years, has been built up an organisation whose thousands of members equip themselves to radiate electrical knowledge.

The Electrical Association for Women was undoubtedly a sorority of believers, a vestal alliance of like-minded devotees dedicated to tending the triple altar of the amp, the volt and the watt, and chanting as one the collective "Ohm" that resonated with the heartbeat of modernity:

> Some of them are women devoting their lives to the creation of a home for their families; some of them are women living alone, cutting down their housework to a minimum in order to devote themselves to other work; some of them are domestic science teachers, spending their lives in equipping the children of to-day for the all-electric world in which they will undoubtedly live to-morrow; some are women employed as demonstrators in the electrical industry, whose work it is to teach others to use electricity adequately. All of them spread the understanding of electricity by preaching it, teaching it, and, above all, using it.

Haslett claimed that electricity was used in 8 million British homes and that two out of every three "housewives" were using it. Yet she urged us all never to forget that there was "a world of difference between the house that is lit, and the home that is run by electricity". As an ambassadress for the cause she had been lauded some years earlier in *The Electrical Handbook for Women* by no less a luminary than Sir John Snell, GBE, M. Inst. CE, MIEE, Chairman, Electricity Commission, 1920–1938:

> As a means of bringing to the knowledge of British housewives the many ways in which

electricity can serve them in reducing drudgery, providing leisure for other things besides keeping the house comfortable and clean, and generally in raising domestic work to an altogether higher status, I know of no organisation which has done so much as the Electrical Association for Women under the inspiring influence and remarkable enterprise of Miss Caroline Haslett, assisted by her band of enthusiastic and able workers.

Teach Yourself Household Electricity is nothing if not practical. Part 1 explains the technicalities of electricity, its generation and distribution, wiring, circuitry – and how to deal with electric shock – but Part 2 looks at the domestic implications (the title of the book, after all) of this wondrous source of power:

This book is written for all interested in electrical methods of home-making. Its aim is to increase the number of enlightened consumers of current to add to the vast army of women who use electricity for lighting, heating, cooking, water-heating, cleaning, washing, ironing, food production and preservation, to whom Christmas and birthdays are occasions upon which family gifts are invariably of the electric variety.

The ritual of Yuletide present-giving in the Haslett household did not bear thinking about.

The psychological benefits of the "all-electric home"

A woman with electrical labour-saving apparatus in her home has time to go out, to take an interest in the affairs of the community, and, if she is so disposed, to play her part in the social and political work of her town. Her wireless keeps her up-to-date, and sharpens her intellect. The improved mental health of women with all-electric homes would make a fascinating subject of research; perfect mental poise renders its owner mistress of any situation.

Teach Yourself Household Electricity, 1939

Although there was no conclusive proof, there were objective indicators that the country was indeed becoming more electricity conscious. According to figures printed in the book, "over a million women" were using electric cookers, "at least 196,000" were using wash-boilers, and 357,000 water-heaters had been installed. Two-thirds of British homes were wired and, according to a survey of 5,829 urban working-class homes carried out in 1934, 5,547 had cookers, 4,390 had wash-boilers, 2,585 had irons, 2,041 had kettles, 1,585 had water heaters, 32 had vacuum cleaners, and 5 had washing machines.

And – if your eyes aren't becoming too heavy by now – a show of hands at "a lecture and symposium on 'Electricity in the Home' given to members of 'a Women's Organisation in South-west London'" – wake up at the back – revealed that "a vacuum cleaner, which saves dust, dirt, and personal fatigue, was the most helpful piece of electrical apparatus a woman could possess, and that, from a labour-saving point of view, a vacuum cleaner came first; with a constant supply of hot water a close second".

Next, Haslett, who by now was beginning to display every impression (erroneous, of course) of being a deep-cover propagandist for some shadowy electrical retailers' cartel, devotes a whole chapter to the thousand and one electrical devices on sale – more than a couple of them bearing eloquent testimony to the depth and persistence of human folly.

Alphabetically, we are introduced to such domestic must-haves as bed-warmers and boiling-rings, breakfast cookers and buffet appliances, car mats and cigarette lighters, dish washers and drying cupboards, egg-cookers and fans, footwarmers and gongs ("it is easy to differentiate between visitor and meal-time indications, by giving a double press for the gong"), hair curling apparatus and mixer-beaters, morning-tea apparatus and plate-warmers, polishers and porringers ("water-jacketed pans in which not only porridge but various other foods, like sauces and custards, can be prepared"), snack-cookers and, intriguingly, stimulators (see Figure 4), steamers and, for the man who has everything apart from a frontal lobe to the brain, tie-irons. After the trouser-press and the pleat-presser we are finally introduced to the vibrator and the waffle iron! "The purpose of an electric vibrator", by the way, "is to massage the skin". One wonders how the electricity lecture and symposium-goers in southwest London (or elsewhere, for that matter) would have voted if asked to rank the relative merits of the vibrator and the waffle-iron. Sadly, on this one, Haslett lacks the data.

Figure 4 The Stimulator, one of the many devices designed to meet a woman's 'electrical needs'.
Teach Yourself Household Electricity, 1939

A COUNTRY AT WAR

It is a lasting compliment to the Teach Yourself series that its content was not trimmed by the war. In 1939 when *Teach Yourself about the Greeks* appeared, for example, eighteen books were on the backlist and the general success of the project was a guarantee that many more would soon join them. As well as *The Student's Guide*, *The Speaker and Debater*, *Bell's Standard Elocutionist*, and *The Household Doctor*, there were volumes on French, Mathematics, Embroidery, Good English, Latin, German, Cookery, Chemistry, Flying, Gardening, Carpentry, and Spanish – an eclectic range of titles in only two years and, so it would prove, a firm foundation for more.

J. C. Stobbart's survey of ancient Greek life, literature and culture was a bold and confident addition to the series, determined to spread the light of civilisation at the very time the Nazis were trying to extinguish it. Just as men and women could forget the realities of war for a time by dreaming of cultivating a herbaceous border, so the more cerebral could find solace from contemporary uncertainties in the beauty that was Greece:

> Hellas provides a thousand objects which seventy-five generations of people have agreed to call beautiful and which no person outside a madhouse has ever thought ugly. The proper use of true classics is to keep them for a compass in the cross-currents of fashion. By

them you may know what is permanent and essential from what is showy and exciting.

Or, as Elsie E. Herron writes in her introduction to the book:

> For, last of all, it is good to know about the Greeks because they were a fine and happy people, and to share their life is to breathe the "pure serene" of a clearer air than ours. The glory of Greece lives still for those who love it.

Alongside the arts and the humanities, however, titles like *Teach Yourself Chemistry* (1938) flew the flag for the sciences and combined, as usual, seriousness with approachability. Concentration and application were vital to the acquisition of knowledge, of course, and it was taken as read that these qualities could be practised in every household regardless of social class or income. However, the book also took it for granted that huge financial outlay was impractical and planned the content accordingly. Anyone feeling that progress in chemistry was barred to someone not in possession of a laboratory to rival that of Dr Frankenstein, for example, needed have no such qualms for reassurance was always at hand:

> Detailed lists of apparatus are easily procurable from the different dealers in scientific fittings, but the ordinary layman, who wishes simply to verify what he has been reading, will find that a few tubes and flasks to stand heat, supplemented by an odd tumbler

or plate from the pantry, will be apparatus enough to repeat some of the most striking and instructive experiments of Davy or Faraday.

That other "application of chemistry", photography, became the subject of the next wave of Teach Yourself titles in 1940 and, following the by now established tradition of the series, refused to let the circumstances of war interrupt the progress of learning.

Odd perhaps that people were thinking about taking snaps and developing them under the stairs while their relatives and friends were fighting abroad. But really no odder than the juxtaposition of other disparate events the world over in 1940 – Churchill making his "Finest Hour" speech in June, for example, followed by Bugs Bunny making his first cartoon appearance on screen in July. The Teach Yourself editors knew that life – "one damn thing after another" – was a moving kaleidoscope of random events and that photography was as much a part of that kaleidoscope as the German invasion of Denmark. On balance, a rather more positive part, too. Stanley Bowler's introduction to the subject begins in a characteristically romantic way:

As we go through life we gather impressions and memories, but inevitably, whether grave or gay, those memories fade from our minds as further experiences claim our attention. To this age, however, has been vouchsafed the priceless opportunity of reserving some of those happy memories of happenings and of people, in a form which is more permanent than many human lives. That is how I like to think of the simple "snap" – a link with the pleasurable past.

What follows is a fairly straightforward though comprehensive introduction to the subject of photography, culminating in a recommendation, the gist of which appears time and again in the series. The beginner is strongly advised to join his or her local photographic society where "you will meet other enthusiasts who are working on the same lines as you".

In Teach Yourself thinking, the society and the club were the ways to proficiency in every sphere. The book would give you the rudiments; the club would give you the practice – and much more besides. Clubs and societies were the backbone of vibrant communities, sharing information and expertise and providing endless social opportunities for men and women of like-minded passions. Indeed, these clubs were themselves communities in miniature, uniting men and women from many different walks of life. They provided an inexpensive and innocent form of entertainment that, viewed from the early twenty-first century, seems to have largely vanished. The clichéd rebuke to the archetypal bored child or teenager, "In my day we made our own amusement", dates from just such an age, an age when clubs and societies criss-crossed the land and there was no excuse for being bored or idle. *O tempora, O mores.*

To just such a distant time belongs a title like *Teach Yourself Biology* (1940), which suggests helpfully:

> Many busy people will be content to "teach themselves biology" by merely reading what is written in a book. Others who have more time or a more inquiring mind, will like to see for themselves, and for their guidance suggestions are made in the following pages for carrying out simple experiments and instructions are given for dissections that can easily be done at home.

It is not just the word "dissection" that might cause some of us to move uneasily in our seats today. "Easily" and "at home" are arguably a shade uncomfortable, too. But in 1940 things were different:

> One all-too-common mammal is the rat, and, for the sake of cheapness, it is often used in dissection. It is, however, an unpleasant animal to deal with, and a little obnoxious to most of us. A rabbit is more expensive, but is much pleasanter to operate upon. A rabbit bought from a poulterer is not a good "subject", for, whether it has been trapped or shot, certain vital parts will have been injured. The best course is to buy, from a recognised dealer in biological material, a rabbit that has been chloroformed.

Er ... yes. Moving on.

Teach Yourself Biology took the idea of the test paper a step further and shrewdly incorporated it into both the reader's study and into the company's marketing strategy. It was undoubtedly an attractive selling point and, for a modest outlay, gave the English Universities Press an attractive and highly persuasive sales gimmick:

> As an added incitement to progress, we have asked the authors to set a Test Paper which will be a challenge to your skill. If you decide to try your hand, send in your paper to the English Universities Press. To all who reach fifty per cent we shall award a copy of the Black Jacket edition of Attilio Gatti's *Great Mother Forest*. If you write an exceptionally good paper, it will be marked 'distinction' and you will be awarded a copy of Professor Goldschmidt's fascinating book *Ascaris; The Biologist's Story of Life* in addition to the 'pass' award. This Test Paper is not in any sense an 'official' examination. It is designed simply to add to your interest in the task of teaching yourself Biology.

It was a brilliant stroke. The reader would be treated like a sixth-former in receipt of a school prize – or even a student preparing for finals – and the company could boast a promotional coup. A couple of books from the warehouse would cost them nothing and a lunch for the markers could be set against tax. It would have been a lunch almost certainly, by the way, not a monetary reward. This was a publishing house, after all. "Good God, man, we wouldn't insult you with cash. Now, you must try the fish."

MIND YOUR LANGUAGE

Concern for clear and effective self-expression always figured high on the Teach Yourself list of priorities. *Teach Yourself to Write* (1942) was a classic of its type:

> Aldous Huxley, questioned on how to become a writer, recommended buying pen, paper, and a bottle of ink – sound advice, indeed, but so bald as to be unhelpful.

Such an irony bypass in the first sentence suggests a shaky start could be followed by a bumpy flight and a crash landing. Not only that. Having put down Aldous Huxley in the first paragraph the author goes on, in short order, to contradict Dr Johnson:

> No sensible person ever writes solely for money ...

... but let us give R. G. Betterton the benefit of the doubt:

> This book is designed for those who, having made their purchase, sit with pen poised wondering where to begin.

However, faced with the possibility of public complaint that teaching yourself to write was an indulgence (and quite possibly a waste of paper) in wartime, the publishers took the precaution of positioning prominently on the dedication page a "Book Production War Economy Standard" badge. The badge – open book topped by lion couchant – reassured potential detractors that "This book is produced in complete conformity with the Authorised Economy Standards." So there.

To business:

> Writing as a pastime has everything to recommend it. It can bring you infinite pleasure, even if your magnum opus has but one admiring reader – yourself. At the least, it is less expensive than bridge, more stimulating than knitting, less exhausting than golf.

You had to hand it to the man. Having offended Aldous Huxley and Dr Johnson, he then goes for the hat-trick by alienating Winifred Butler (*Teach Yourself Knitting*, 1979).

You, too, can be a writer.

Live as fully as possible, seeking new experiences, making new friends, keeping all your faculties open to the ceaseless activity of life. The would-be writer should move freely in the world, should walk and talk and argue and, in short, embrace all experience, painful or pleasant, that will enlarge his heart and understanding.

Teach Yourself to Write, 1942

In his first chapter on style ("not the coat of varnish but the grain in the wood"), Betterton commendably praises original writing as the surest test of original thought:

Leave the cliché, the windy circumlocution, the dead metaphor to the tired after-dinner speaker or the fifth-rate politician, who must needs use them to fill up the interstices of thought or conceal the fact that he is incapable of original thinking. When you find yourself writing to all intents and purposes, through thick and thin, through fire and water, when you seek to rivet the attention, explore every avenue, apply the acid test, then it is time for you to put down your pen and reconsider what you have written.

And, at the end of the day, this advice *was* sound stuff.

Following the now established pattern of including test papers in the book, the publishers set readers a series of writing exercises – this time without keys and answers but to encourage them to keep up their practice. As with *Teach Yourself Biology*, a test paper was included, although intriguingly it was scaled down to the status of "competition" and a prize offered:

> If you decide to try your hand, send in your entry to the English Universities Press ...

... and ...

> To all who reach fifty per cent we shall send the award of *a* book. [author's italics]

Was there no end to the publishers' generosity?

A KALEIDOSCOPE OF TITLES

"Would you build a house without foundations?" wondered *Teach Yourself Algebra* rhetorically in 1942:

> Of course the answer is 'No!' Neither can you, without Algebra, acquire a sound knowledge of any branch of Mathematics, with the possible exception of Geometry. If you would understand thoroughly Trigonometry or mechanics, or the Calculus, or any of their applications, you must have a basis of Algebra.

Make sure of your foundations!

There was something of the grumpy schoolmaster in its approach, it has to be said; a bossy tone that expected everyone to pull their socks up and look lively. But equally it could also have been construed as a form of enthusiasm, certainly a sense of urgency that there was a world of study out there just waiting to be pursued. The publishers sensed they were on to a winner with the series and it is just possible that a degree of stridency had replaced its merely self-confident tone.

In the same year, *Teach Yourself to Draw* appeared on the shelves with a reference (frequently and irritatingly copied by many titles) to the precedent set by early man:

> We know that, some twenty thousand years before Christ, the cave-dweller returning from his hunting would spend the dark hours painting and drawing on the rough walls of his home, helped perhaps by the flickering light from a fire, intensely observed pictures of the animals he had slain and of those which had eluded him.

> We know, too, that there are among us today some who return home from very different work in the city, factory, or field, and find the same satisfaction and a great deal of healthy "release" in leisure hours spent with pencil and brush.

Hyperbole was not dead. And it was comforting to know we were the direct descendants of the Flintstones and heirs to their artistic achievements.

Some of the emerging Teach Yourself volumes were practical, some were theoretical, but all claimed to be, in their varying degrees, relevant to the society of their time. Take *Teach Yourself Bee-keeping*, for example:

> During the present war the value of sugar, and commodities containing sugar, have been more appreciated by the general public than in years of peace. It is not surprising therefore that many thousands have turned to the most ancient means of producing sweetening material, namely, the keeping of the honey-bee.

Or *Teach Yourself Geology*:

> To call a person "an old fossil" conjures up a picture of a more or less inoffensive old man, a little musty, out of date in his thinking, and very unprogressive. It is a term of kindly tolerance mixed with pity and criticism. This picture would represent the attitude of many of the public to the science of geology, regarding it as a subject very remote from daily life, a suitable subject for the entertainment of absent-minded professors. Geology is the antithesis of all this – it has a vital contribution that is being made daily to our

everyday life and comfort in a thousand and one different contacts, no less real because they are not obvious.

A quaintly antique tone hovers above the books from this period, lending volumes on everyday trades, such as bricklaying, a solemn and schoolmasterly air:

> A brick is best described as "a building unit". The shape and convenient size of a brick enables a man to grip it with an easy confidence and, because of this, brick-building has been popular for many hundreds of years. The hand of the average man is sufficiently large to span the width of a brick and the arrangement of a man's hand and arm is such that he is able to handle more than 500 bricks in an eight-hour day.

After a brief survey of mortar and its constituent parts of lime mix, Portland cement, and sand, in his section titled "Details of a Brick" E. L. Braley soberly intones:

> The opportune moment has now arrived to discuss bricks more fully and become intimately acquainted with them.

For most of us a brick is a brick but for Mr Braley it is far more than that – as an "isometric sketch and an orthographic projection" of a brick (Plate I, see Figure 5) make clear. *Teach Yourself Brickwork* (1944), in common with all the other books in the

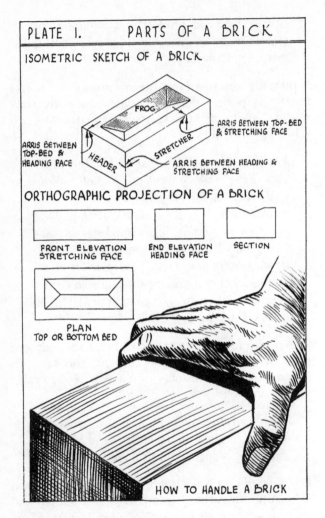

Figure 5 *Teach Yourself Brickwork*, 1944

series, prided itself on its thoroughness and it was fascinating to be introduced to the intricacies of a trade by a master craftsman supremely confident in his own talents. In Braley's hands the everyday brick became an object of fascination, an arcane thing of beauteous simplicity that slowly gave up its mysteries with the turning of each page.

Similarly, the action of picking up mortar on the trowel may seem simple enough to the uninitiated, but to a master it was a precise action, as complex as a movement from Tai Chi, requiring the skill of an athlete coupled with the subtle dexterity of a martial artist:

> Before attempting to lay a brick one must learn how to pick up a trowelful of mortar. This will prove most difficult of achievement. To obtain proficiency in this subject a great deal of practice is essential. For it is only by actually going through the motions that the wrist will become supple, the stabilising degree of balance be sensed, the correct hold of the trowel developed, and the strength of the grip required to hold the mortar on to the trowel be ascertained.

This decorous tone also extends to the otherwise prosaic action of cutting a brick in two with a brick-hammer:

> By holding the brick firmly upon the left leg, just above the knee-cap, so that the shock of the impact is taken up by the femur, a fairly

comfortable and comparatively safe position may be found in which to cut the brick.

Note, too, how Braley discreetly deals with potential mis-hits which even in the more sedate atmosphere of 1944 would surely prompt a vocalised expletive on the building site:

> It must, however, be borne in mind that the blow from a brick-hammer is a vicious one; and if, inadvertently, the hand or leg is hit, the memory of it will remain a long time.

No, in the expletive-free world of Teach Yourself we may imagine only the following exclamation as the brickie's mate takes a swing with the brick-hammer (brick resting on upper femur as instructed) and misses: "Gosh, the memory of that one will remain with me a long time."

Somehow the gentility of the approach is carried on even in the illustrations, which are rather fine, intricate line drawings clearly labelled in simple calligraphic script and each bearing a plate number in Roman numerals. Perfect.

Teach Yourself Roofing (1944) took its place beside companion volumes – *Brickwork*, *Constructional Details*, *Planning and Design*, *Joinery Plumbing*, *Quantity Surveying*, *House Repairs*, and *Electricity in the House* – and together they formed the "*Teach Yourself Building*" series-within-a-series.

"This small book tells briefly the story of the roof; how it is constructed and how it is covered," reads the preface of *Teach Yourself Roofing* with commendable clarity. And the story of the roof, in shorthand, is sketched out in the opening paragraph from primitive man (predictably) in the "solid protection of a cave" to his development of "skin tents" and simple timber constructions of wattle and daub topped first with stone slabs then later with "specially made tiles".

We learn that the Greeks used marble tiles to cover their temples and that the Romans used clay tiles for their houses – the flat tile known as the "tegula", the round tile known as the "imbrex". And finally we enjoy a brisk canter through the use of thatch, slate, corrugated iron ("objectionable" because of appearance, rust and noise) and various cement and concrete products. It is a masterly summary bringing us right up to date (and face to face with the realities of the times). On first-aid repairs, for example, J. Lee says:

> When bombing takes place in a town, the task
> of making houses habitable, and warehouses
> and factories capable of immediate use, is of
> first-rate importance.

If we should ever need a roofer today, how we should long for a man who knows his "imbrex" from his "tegula". How we should long, in fact, for J. Lee, a craftsman at the top of his trade, supremely confident that nothing he could encounter at roof level could surprise or defeat him.

POST-WAR THINKING

In the summer of 1944, the Allies launched their D-Day landings on the beaches of Northern France. In Amsterdam, the Gestapo closed in on Anne Frank in her attic room, later deporting her, via Auschwitz, to Bergen-Belsen concentration camp. In England, however, optimism seemed almost mandatory with J. E. Macfarlane (*Teach Yourself Electricity in the House*, 1944) looking to post-war reconstruction and "the provision of large numbers of new houses":

> Light, airy houses will be popular after the dingy black-out conditions of war-time, and every effort must be made to take full advantage of all amenities in the new construction. Electricity is an essential portion of the modern house, and due thought must be given to its inclusion to give a harmonious whole and not as an item to be added as an afterthought.

If you wanted to get the measure of at least Mr Macfarlane's optimism, one glance at his plans for a detached house would have done the trick (see Figure 6). Three bedrooms, a bathroom, and a sewing room upstairs complemented the dining room, kitchen, music room, study, hall, garage, wash house, and tool-shed below. Just the thing for the tenement dweller to aspire to. Although this was certainly not typical of wartime expectations,

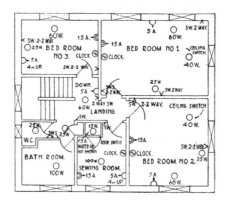

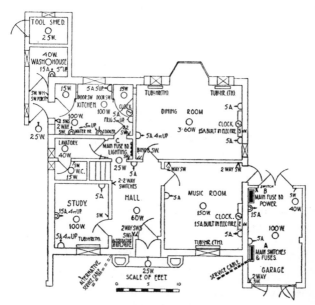

Figure 6 *Teach Yourself Electricity in the House*, 1944

the photographs of idealised (if, by our standards, spartan) interiors gave every impression that the good life was just around the corner.

Teach Yourself to Express Yourself (1944) saw the return of the irrepressible R. W. Jepson, author of *Teach Yourself to Think* (1938). A headmaster by profession, he adopted a correspondingly schoolmasterly tone throughout, alienating, one now feels, as many readers as he sought to attract. Yet his general claim that clear, concise, correct and coherent English is at the root of good communication still stands. Moreover, in promoting its use in all stations and classes of society he became a sort of standard bearer of the meritocracy we would see emerging in the 1950s.

Strange, though, that, having praised concision, he could have brought himself to write a sentence like this:

> Just as careful pruning, by removing dead and superfluous wood and by letting in light and air, strengthens the growth and stimulates the bearing power of fruit-trees, so if you cut out superfluous words and other unnecessary or irrelevant excrescences or encumbrances, your writing will be stronger and healthier.

Four out of ten for that, maestro.

Nevertheless, for all that, the book was a positive contribution to the technicalities of good expression, persuading readers to look at words and phrases in a more critical light and to ask themselves whether, quite simply, they could find a better way of saying the same thing. As a personal take on one aspect of the English language it was a minor *Eats, Shoots & Leaves* (2003) of its day – which, as we all know, went on to be a million-dollar best-seller. The Teach Yourself people were definitely on to something. And they knew it.

THE TUNNEL'S END

In the circumstances of the war we have all found ourselves doing new and unexpected things. Civilians have become soldiers, sailors and airmen. Women have entered the Services or are doing men's work in factories. The oldest and the youngest have studied first-aid, anti-gas technique and the ways of incendiary bombs; or they have learned to rear poultry or rabbits, or to regulate their own diets on scientific principles.

Teach Yourself to Study, 1945

With the above paragraph, Dr G. G. Neill Wright began his opening chapter on the changing nature of society. The fact that the British population had learned so much in times of war was proof for him that we could learn much more in times of peace. Possibilities for self-improvement were endless:

> The post-war world will not be Utopia, but it may
> well be an improvement on the pre-war world,
> for we have learned so much to which, before the
> war, we shut our eyes and minds. The extent to
> which it will be an improvement depends largely
> upon ourselves, upon our ability to learn the
> lessons of our experience, and to see and make
> use of the opportunities which will be open to us.

And the Teach Yourself books were nothing if not committed to opening up opportunities. As a Teach Yourself author, Dr Wright *would* have said the following, wouldn't he? Though, even at this distance, it feels unprompted and from the heart:

> There is now no important branch of
> knowledge that cannot be studied in cheap
> manuals written by competent scholars, which
> make learning easy, and such are reaching a
> wider public every day.

Dr Wright had begun the chapter on "A Changing Society" with a quotation from Alexander Pope. Although the proverbial man in the street had probably never read it, he could certainly now, courtesy even of the book he was holding in his hand, understand the sentiment:

> Late as it is, I put myself to school,
> And feel some comfort not to be a fool.

Teach Yourself had taken off. Its boosters had propelled it beyond the earth's atmosphere and it was on course "to infinity and beyond".

CHAPTER II

SUNLIT UPLANDS

1940s

Give Instruction to a wise man and he will be yet wiser.

The Bible, Proverbs 9:9

The Bible quotation that was included on the end papers of every Teach Yourself book was probably ignored by most readers as they plunged headlong into their study of French or philosophy, antique collecting or golf. Yet had they considered it for a moment, they would have been flattered. It did not say, for instance, "Give instruction to a fathead or ignoramus and you will make him wise." No. The assumption was that readers were already wise. True, they may have known nothing about horse management or Alexander the Great at the outset but they knew *that they did not know* and they knew *that they wanted to know* – and therein lay the seeds of wisdom.

The nature of the challenge

People who buy a book on English Grammar already know that a sound knowledge of the grammar of their own language will give them greater confidence in speaking and writing. Those who are content to be inarticulate do not try to improve either their speech or their writing. But those who are ambitious to make the most of the opportunities life offers them, want to say and write what is in their minds so that everyone can understand what they mean.

Teach Yourself English Grammar, 1944

Teaching and learning became a shared endeavour, with both teacher and student respectful of each other. Or, as J. C. Kingsland and W. B. Cornish put it in *Teach Yourself Geography* (1939):

> One of the fundamental principles of all good
> teaching and good learning is that there should
> be constant interplay of ideas between teacher
> and taught. A good teacher is not content
> merely to lecture. He questions his pupils, sets
> them problems, and as far as may be he helps
> them to teach themselves.

That was, and still is, the Teach Yourself ethos in a
nutshell. First give beginners a respectful welcome
with full acknowledgement of their desire to learn
something new, then gently introduce them to the
subject by explaining its history and background,
before taking them further and further into the
detail while setting questions and tests along the
way. For two shillings and sixpence it was, by any
objective standards, pretty good value for money.
Not least because the authors and publishers
sincerely believed that education, as a commodity,
was priceless.

The large number of titles already available on
subjects as diverse as trigonometry and roofing
was evidence of the publishers' commitment to
education in its broadest sense. Whatever else they
might have been accused of they could not have
been accused of intellectual snobbery or academic
elitism. For every book on English grammar or
Latin there was one on photography or
dressmaking.

There was one subject area, however, that was
targeted specifically at one sector of the population
– farmers. In the late 1930s, largely driven by the
Daily Express newspaper, a campaign had been

Figure 7 *Teach Yourself Good Milk Farming*, 1946
Illustration by Barbara Dominy

launched to grow more food, partly to rescue British agriculture from the doldrums and partly to ensure that the country would no longer be dependent on foreign food imports. Sensing a potential market, the Teach Yourself publishers sought the active co-operation of London University's Wye College and, in 1943, a "Teach Yourself Farming" series was launched.

THE NOBILITY OF TOIL

The farming series got off to a brilliant start with *Teach Yourself Good Farm Workmanship* (1944), which had the inspired idea of persuading Donald Fletcher, a busy and successful farmer with experience of farming in Yorkshire and Kent, to take the reader on a tour of an imaginary farm, introducing them to the various workmen along the way.

The editors of the series recognised that actual farm visits were a standard feature of the agricultural college curriculum but that, as publishers, they could not hope to replicate them. Instead they proposed (long before the word had been coined) a "virtual" farm tour with Fletcher as guide. But what a guide:

> Here is a *real* farmer talking to you. Some of the things he tells you may bring a frown to the brow of the theorist, a frown of disagreement; some of his practices may not meet with the approval of the scientist; but here, at least, are the ideas of a *real* farmer telling you his experiences in his own words.

And as things turned out, Farmer Fletcher was a natural storyteller with a winning way of describing his work to the layman and specialist alike, and had the knack of talking to the reader as if they were an eager young nephew for whom he had a soft spot. And as he took the reader on this imaginary journey around Mr Bishop's farm, they could hear the sounds, see the sights, and smell the smells of a working farm whose like has disappeared forever. It was a delightful stroll through a long vanished world in the company of a man who "excluding schooldays and soldiering days" had spent "a large part of fifty years on the land".

Fletcher was a friendly and unassuming guide, teeming with understated wisdom. As he took readers around the farm, he not only instructed them but let them into little secrets in throwaway asides that revealed more than any other formal tutor could; how he had made mistakes and was still making them; how farming could be monotonous if your heart wasn't in it; how he had a sneaking fondness for gypsies because of their obvious love for their horses, dogs and, on one occasion, cats:

> For my part, I am quite prepared to overlook many shortcomings in a man who takes good care of an animal. One of these same gypsies had a pet cat, wore a poacher's coat with a large inside coat and, wherever he went, puss was always carried about in this pocket where she seemed perfectly happy. He even used to

Figure 8 *Teach Yourself Good Market Gardening*, 1948

take the cat to the local inn where he went for his share of good cheer. When he worked in the fields during the day, he took off the famous coat, fished puss out, and laid her out on the coat in the sunshine. She used to sleep there all day and kept strict guard over her master's property until work stopped.

A digression, perhaps, but a delightful one and a story you would probably not have heard in an agricultural college lecture room.

However, despite the lightness of touch, there was solid information to be had. First we meet Jack Sharp, "head cowman in charge of a dairy herd of fifty cows". He was a specialist and knew his job from "A to Z". And because he was a good cowman we could assume that Jack's employer was a first-class farmer because:

Jack is most certainly not the type of man to stay on a farm which is not properly managed. Good masters and good men generally go together.

In this timeless world that is slow to change and whose order is fixed, we follow Jack through his morning ritual:

Jack's alarm clock nearly splits his eardrums as it goes off with a bang at 5 am ... His house is only 50 yards from the byre so he is soon on the job ... Luckily this farm has electric light. A flick of the switch and the cowshed is as bright as day ... Jack has not seen the cows since 9 pm the previous night ... He then starts to give them breakfast, a mixture of some concentrated food such as bran, oats, and oil-cake ... Jack stops at each stall and rations out the correct quantity.

Along the way we learn the duties of the cowman, the tricks of his trade, and those bits of farming practice that only Jack (aka Donald Fletcher himself) could have picked up in a lifetime of work on the farm.

Next we are introduced to Ned Trumper, the shepherd, who will tell us in person all we need to know about tail-cutting and castration, blow-fly attack and intestinal worm infestation, sheep shearing, wool disposal, and treatment for foot rot. Nice to know that being a townie has its advantages sometimes.

After that, 18-year-old Henry Philips makes his appearance. Henry "comes as a young man to Mr Bishop's farm in 1926 and leaves it as a skilled and accomplished pigman to take up the managership of a pig farm in 1938". Henry will explain the layout of the piggeries, the routine of pig-keeping on a general farm, and the minutiae of feeding, rationing and mating. He will tell us about weighing and fattening pigs and how to deal with problems such as "swine-erysipelas".

Next up, in a cast list that reads like a script from "The Archers", is Bill Lyon the wagoner, who will offer general hints on the management of horses, demonstrate the practicalities of feeding and fitting the harness, and outline how the day's ploughing is going to proceed. He will talk knowledgably about feeding and watering after work and explain the intricacies of harrowing, drilling and horse-hoeing. Once he has offered a few tips about how to right a horse that has been pulling a loaded cart and slipped on ice, and about what to do if a horse is stuck in a muddy stream, Fletcher chips in with the following to round off another informative chapter:

> Before the war, the horse population on the land in Great Britain was gradually diminishing. Some say that the days of the horse are numbered and that mechanization will eventually provide more economic power for every kind of job. That day has most certainly not arrived yet! From the sentimental point of view there must be very few farmers or farm workers who will not deplore the arrival of such a day and the passing of one of the finest animals in creation.

Then we come to George Green, the tractor driver who is emphatically not the "man wearing very oily overalls who simply sits on his machine as it goes across a field and back again pulling a plough". No, there is more to the tractor driver's work and the author allows George to make this clear. Thorough familiarity with all the farm's implements, a knowledge of how soil and weather will affect their settings and adjustments, plus hair-trigger judgements about how much can be ploughed in a day are just some of the skills he needs to have at hand.

The farm as an interdependent unit

George Green is ploughing with his tractor. Two fields away are the sheep. He sees one of the sheep on its back. It cannot get up. Does he think, 'Oh – that's Ned's job, let it stay where it is until Ned comes'? Of course, he does not. He would be looked upon as a pretty poor type of fellow if he did. Or again, it is harvest time and the weather is unsettled. Work must go on til dark. Does Jack Sharp say, 'Not for me. I'm head cowman here. Harvest is no concern of mine.'? Rather not. He turns out after tea with everyone else. In short a farm is a unit which cannot easily be sub-divided into water-tight compartments. It is the farm as a whole that counts.

Teach Yourself Farm Workmanship, 1944

In introducing detailed (and potentially technical and/or tedious) information in such a lively and engaging way, the Teach Yourself editors had hit on an attractive style. And in Fletcher, it has to be said, they had found a minor genius. It had to be too good to be true. Although the publishers went on to produce competent and instructive volumes

Figure 9 *Teach Yourself Good Market Gardening*, 1948

written in clear and simple English by locally and nationally acclaimed experts, no single book quite equalled Fletcher's for sheer readability.

Style aside, the farming series was an important milestone in the reversal of fortunes of British agriculture. Champions like V. C. Fishwick (*Teach Yourself Good Farming*, 1944) did their best to tell the general public of the debt the nation owed to its farmers:

> Twice in our time British farmers have helped to save the nation from disaster. Both in the 1914–19 and 1939 world wars the U-boat menace was only defeated by the combined efforts of the sailor and the farmer.

Fishwick explains how, at the outbreak of both wars, Britain was dependent on essential foods from abroad, how the Royal Navy, extended to the limit, was unable to ensure their safe importation into the country, and how, in his view, "this country was only saved from starvation ... by increased production by our own farms".

What he lacks in Fletcher's style he compensates for in hard-nosed statistics:

> Between 1939 and 1943 four million acres of pasture were ploughed up and added to the area under arable cultivation, by the latter year the home farms were producing nearly the whole of our bread corn, and practically all the domestic sugar ration, whilst the milk supply has been maintained largely on home grown

feeding stuffs, and an adequate supply of
potatoes and essential vegetable and fruit has
been produced.

**Five ways to regenerate the agricultural
industry**

1. Improved pay and conditions for farm
   workers (who, in March 1943, were on a
   minimum weekly wage of £3).
2. Improvement in rural housing at a time
   when very few villages had an electricity,
   gas, or water, supply.
3. Increased availability of secondary
   education for village children.
4. The provision of social centres in the
   form of a village hall.
5. The development of better rural
   transport.

Teach Yourself Good farming, 1944

In this no-nonsense approach to farming practice,
Fishwick made an important contribution to
understanding what it took to be an efficient and
productive farmer in wartime and post-war Britain.
What the series was at pains to explode was the
fallacy that "farming is a way of life rather than a
business". Those behind the farming books, on the
contrary, believed it was a business in which
efficiency was essential to success.

Teach Yourself Good Farm Crops (1944) was written in the same vein – with a title page and subject breakdown that read like Charles Dickens's chapter synopsis from *Oliver Twist*:

GOOD FARM CROPS

wherein are displayed and fully annotated for the benefit of all interested in those modern methods which will enable a farmer to produce from his soils good food for man and beast with directions for preparing the seed, manuring, liming, tilling, draining, irrigating and reclaiming various lands according to the best and most up-to-date practices as well as shewing how good crops can even be raised on bad land together with other matters useful to the husbandman ingeniously set forth by

A. W. OLDERSHAW

sometime Agricultural Organizer for East Suffolk The Whole made still more intelligible to the reader by numerous illustrations prepared from sketches by

Agnes Oldershaw

Quite a sentence! One sentence, in fact. Mr Oldershaw began on a slightly petulant note:

For the moment agriculture stands high in the nation's esteem. It should do, for it has filled and is filling bellies that would otherwise be empty. It is no mean boast that today 70% of the food we eat comes from the fields of this small island, despite of the vast areas, usually of our most productive land, that have perforce been requisitioned for military purposes.

Corn crops, root crops, forage and grazing crops all got his full attention as he explained the best techniques for maximising the yield from what had the potential to be our "exceedingly fertile and fruitful" country. He was aware that the reconstruction of the agricultural industry "when the War is over and victory is won" would be a long job but, for him, it was a vital task to perform and one whose aim was twofold; to provide workers with decent pay and conditions and to give farmers and farm owners an adequate return on their hard work and skill. Get those things right, he believed, and the industry would flourish once again because "it is very important from the point of view of the future of the nation that a hardy and healthy race should be maintained upon the land".

It was a passionately argued book written by a man steeped in the farming industry. This was clear from the outset in a personal and rather moving dedication that alone established his competence far more than any academic title or degree could have done. It read simply:

To my
FATHER and MOTHER
who lived at
Glebe farm, Costock
Nottinghamshire
For
44 years

Good Farm Accounting

Wherein are exhibited not only the value and importance of recording all farm transactions but also those simple methods by which the busy farmer can keep the necessary books connected with his business, illustrated by adequate examples together with such tables and particulars as are essential to tranquility of mind and clear reckoning in the midst of an exacting and industrious life.

Title page of *Teach Yourself Good Farm Accounting*, 1945

Books like these – indeed the farming series as a whole – did their not inconsiderable bit to help bolster production. Cheap, easy to read, distinctly packaged with a reassuringly bucolic image on every cover, these were perfect books to have on the farmhouse bookshelves, and ones that it is easy to imagine farmers consulting when necessary. Not least because they would have known that every book had been written, in effect, by one of their own kind who actually knew what he was talking about.

SPEED THE PLOUGH

What Donald Fletcher had feared in 1944 (but must have known in his heart was inevitable) came nearer to reality 1948 when *Teach Yourself Good Farming by Machine* first appeared:

> Although domestication of oxen and horses made possible the development of farm implements as we know them to-day, it is likely that the horse, as the provider of farm power, will have become obsolete in a very few years and will have been replaced entirely by the tractor or by some other mechanical means of converting fuel into energy for field cultivation.

Fletcher had hard factual evidence from the recent past that that was the case, quoting the huge increase in tractor ploughmen that had been necessary during the recent war. He noted, too, how members of the Women's Land Army had been successfully drafted in to help boost the workforce, but added this apparently back-handed compliment:

> It is no discredit to the wonderful service these girls rendered, to say that it took them very much longer to become ploughmen than it took the horse-ploughmen to become tractor drivers.

Nonetheless, from a careful reading of the text it is clear that the author had no implied slight in his mind at all. What he meant was that the mechanised side of things was always going to be secondary to the agricultural. In other words, it was always going to be more important that the person doing the ploughing knew more about the soil than about the tractor. And knowing about the soil required years of experience which no beginner (man or woman) could acquire overnight:

> Ploughing needs a knowledge of the soil that can come only from recording in one's mind the behaviour of the soil in all conditions; from remembering how it behaved, and had to be treated, on days when it was so sticky that it would not scour off the face of the mouldboard and on days when it was baked so hard that the plough-share had to be given a special tilt to make it penetrate at all.

It was a fascinating glimpse into the subtleties of working the land that only experience (or a book) could provide. And he could also do without smart-alec comments from in-comers, thank you very much. To those critics who accused farmers of neglecting their machinery, for instance, and letting their chain drives run dry of oil ("which no factory worker would do"), he has this to say:

> This is not because the farmer has forgotten to oil it; he knows that an oil-covered chain, working in a cloud of soil-dust, picks up

abrasive particles which mix with the oil and cause the chain and sprockets to wear out much more quickly than if they were running dry.

So there. And smug townies who thought they knew everything about maintaining machinery and who believed farmers were only just catching up with the age of mechanisation, could put that in their pipes and smoke it.

Insights like this, based on long experience of the practicalities of day-to-day farming, regularly leapt off the pages of all the farming books in the series and could be relied on to surprise and fascinate the non-specialist reader – as well as save the would-be farmer large amounts of wasted time and effort.

"Priority food number one"; the daily pinta

Not only is it a complete food in itself, but its richness in vitamins and most of the minerals and desirable elements contribute to the maintenance of a high standard of health. Medical opinion shares the view that milk consumption should be much increased beyond the 0.4 pints per head per day of the pre-war era.

Teach Yourself Good Milk Farming, 1946

The authors were hardly chosen at random. They were carefully selected by the editors for their expertise in farming (of course) but also for other less definable qualities that contributed to their status and that established them as first rate communicators. Donald Fletcher, as we have seen, was a gifted storyteller and others, like S. G. Jary (*Teach Yourself Good Control of Insect Pests,* 1948), came with a "hinterland", a background of experience and learning that made them stand out from the ordinary.

Jary, for example, was a Cambridge graduate in entomology, an academic, and Government adviser who also, as the series editor informed us in the preface, had "an adventurous career in the first World War as a pilot in the R.A.F." and "managed, somehow, to land when he was shot down by the Germans in the days before parachutes were generally worn". Not just any old run-of-the-mill farmer from Ambridge, then. No, "an authority of first rank".

G. H. Tawell (*Teach Yourself Good Market Gardening,* 1948), though not himself blasted out of the sky by the Germans, was equally qualified in his own field and declares himself, from the outset, to be a no-nonsense kind of individual who expects a no-nonsense attitude from his students:

This is a plain book. There are no frills, there is no oratory. There are no pages that can be skipped because they are mere padding; each chapter is a summary of facts. The reason for this abridgement is that the author is a very

busy man. Moreover he is a practical man who
works all day with his hands – and sometimes
half the night. Practically every page has been
committed to paper after seven o'clock in the
evening because the late hours have been the
only time available.

So much for him. What about you and your
suitability as a potential market gardener? Stand well
back. You are about to experience a gale of reality:

If you are not equipped with good health, a
patient bearing, the capacity for unremitting
work if needs be – then leave it alone!

If, on the other hand, you can, by starting with
a low standard of living, by slogging and
enduring set-backs, gradually improve your
position; if you can do the work of two or three
men because you simply cannot afford to pay
their wages; if you can withstand the sight of the
loss of a field of Brussels sprouts rendered
unsaleable by drought and greenfly, the
ploughing-in of a first-rate stretch of lettuce
because it has run to seed before there is a
market for it; the complete destruction of costly
seedbeds through late frosts or flea-beetle; the
slaughter of every pig on the place at twenty-
four hours' notice owing to swine fever brought
in by the chance settling of a starling in your
yard or carried on the contaminated boots of a
visitor – if you have enough stamina to face all

ills, and petty jealousies, and all set-backs, and start again from scratch, undaunted, rather having benefited than otherwise by the experience, then you are made of the right metal, you have passed the first test. We are ready to proceed.

So a snooze was out of the question. The essentials for the successful market gardener were organisation and drive ("sometimes at the expense of his personal popularity"). Mr Tawell was clearly not an easy man nor one to hold his tongue when he saw signs of slacking in those around him. He was a countryman through and through, with the farmer's suspicion of the city factory worker who clocked in and out of a grindingly monotonous job for which he had no passion or commitment. Contrast this with the farm worker:

> To him an extra half-hour is neither here nor there, if a job has got to be done. To him the thought of striking for higher wages would be foreign to his very nature. The nearer to the towns you get the fewer become these trusties, and it is distressing to witness the irresponsible mentality displayed by many of the youths who come out of the towns to work on nearby farms.

So, nothing's changed, then. Other volumes in the series, from *Teach Yourself Good Soil* (1944) to *Teach Yourself Good Grassland* (1947), from *Teach Yourself Horse Management* (1951) to *Teach Yourself Forestry* (1955), were less censorious in their approach. What all the books had in common, however, was a passionate commitment to their subject matter combined with a down-to-earth readability that made them stand out from other books on similar topics. Taken together, they made up an authoritative library of farming theory and practice, and formed a collection that could sit, one imagined, inconspicuously and unself-consciously on the shelves of every farmhouse in the land.

DON'T MENTION THE WAR

Man did not live for physical toil alone. Noble as it was, there was also the inner life to attend to. In 1946, the Teach Yourself publishers enlisted the support of the historian, Shakespearean scholar, and Fellow of All Souls, Dr A. L. Rowse, to edit a major new project that would do for history what the "Teach Yourself Farming" series had done for agriculture.

The "Teach Yourself History Library" was launched in 1946 by Dr Rowse himself, whose inaugural *Teach Yourself the Use of History* got the series off to the proverbial flying start. The choice of Dr Rowse was inspired. Here was a brilliant and charismatic scholar in the high summer of his powers, known to the public for the sharpness of his wit and for the bold (often controversial) nature of his opinions.

Born to poor labouring parents in Cornwall but, by native talent, inclination and hard work destined for success in one of the most rarefied academic establishments in Europe and the world,

Dr Alfred Leslie Rowse was a complex mixture of the elitist and the populist. In him, academic rigour vied with intellectual arrogance producing a persona which, though to many highly irritating, could not be ignored. Possessed also of a mischievous twinkle in the eye, he was the David Starkey of his day, not quite "the rudest man in Britain" but waspish enough to sting effectively in argument. He was becoming an increasingly well-known public figure and as such qualified as a high-profile name to launch this important new series. He kicked it off in characteristically unequivocal style:

> This series has been undertaken in the conviction that there can be no subject of study more important than history. Great as have been the conquests of natural science in our time – such that many think of ours as a scientific age par excellence – it is even more urgent and necessary that advances should be made in the social sciences, if we are to gain control of the forces of nature loosed upon us. The bed out of which all the social sciences spring is history.

Well placed to sniff out the best and brightest talents in academia (and probably inclined from time to time to exclude quite a few, too, for complex reasons of professional rivalry, personal pique and academic politics), Dr Rowse recruited writers who, above all, he believed, could communicate and inspire:

> I need hardly say that I am a strong believer in people with good academic standards writing

once more for the general reading public, and of the public being given the best that the universities can provide. From this point of view this series is intended to bring the university into the homes of the people.

Note, too, that he (and, by extension, the series as a whole) intended to take the university into the home not the people into university. Teach Yourself set out to appeal to the broadest mass of the people in whatever job, trade or profession and from whatever social background. As if to underline this, Dr Rowse admitted a soft spot for those great popularists of the day – journalists – who were a despised group in the eyes of many a cloistered academic.

By page six, however, Dr Rowse had warmed to his central theme – the use of history and its importance, in particular, in the foreign policy of a country. As an outspoken opponent of appeasement in the Second World War (and in 1946 this was not history but current affairs), he was now in a position to settle a few old scores and to get a few things off his chest. In an unashamed piece of personal invective he writes:

In all the pitiable revelation of a third-rate mind in a front-rank post that is afforded by a reading of Sir Nevile Henderson's *Failure of a Mission* – he was in a key position as British Ambassador in Berlin from 1937 to 1939 – nothing is more deplorable than the ignorance of the man as to the character of the

developments in Germany. Only a little orderly
reading of modern German history would have
given him the clue to them.

Once the point about the use of history had been
made, Dr Rowse could not help himself taking
things to another level of personal abuse:

> But he seems to have thought a reading of
> *Mein Kampf* on board ship from South
> America home was sufficient. No wonder he
> was both fogged and foxed by the direction of
> events in Germany and seems never to have
> grasped it until too late.

It was rumbustious stuff – and hugely entertaining.
Historical contextualisation saved it from being a
naked rant – but only just – and one doubts whether
historical analysis today would be presented in quite
such unvarnished terms. Those of a disposition that
is easily upset should turn away now:

> How can one properly understand the career of
> Hitler and the resurgence of German
> militarism, its undying appeal for the German
> people, if one knows nothing of Bismarck and
> Frederick the Great, of the whole cult of
> militarism, the tradition of German aggression?

There was more to come:

> It ought not to have been so very difficult to
> forecast, on quite a moderate acquaintance
> with the German people and their recent

history, that they would make a second bid for world power. The worst thing that their history reveals, worse than their criminal brutality, their stupidity and insensibility, their sycophancy and self-pity, is their utter lack of any sense of responsibility for what they do – for that is what leads to all the rest.

And more:

After all, aggression is what has always paid in German history. Frederick the Great's career was one long record of successful aggression. So was Bismarck's. The total upshot of Bismarck's irruption upon the scene was to put back the clock a hundred years in European civilisation. Yet Frederick and Bismarck are the two great heroes of politics to the German mind – and likely to remain so. Achtung!

More tea, anyone?

By page ten he was beginning to calm down a bit. But only a bit:

Ignorance in high places, and in particular the absence of any historical understanding of the political developments in Europe, led us in the last ten years as near as anything to disaster. It is all very well for the circles mainly responsible to blame it now, with a kind of mean generosity, upon the people at large. The people were no doubt ignorant: they always

are. But that is no reason why they should
continue to be so. (It is the main purpose of
such a series of books as this to dispel
ignorance, in so far as it can.)

After this, a warning which was direct and personal
– as if from a feared schoolmaster to a class of
sixth-formers of whom much was expected:

If you do not understand the world you live in,
you are merely its sport, and apt to become its
victim. (Most people are that anyway. But that
is no reason why you should be one of them).
In understanding is our only emancipation.

Chapter II saw the author in a much less
confrontational mood, settling down to the subject
at hand – history (should you have forgotten) – and
examining in quirky and always entertaining detail
its many and various aspects. Having explored its
utilitarian aspect he turns to the simple intellectual
satisfaction to be had from historical analysis (thus,
incidentally, prefiguring by eight years the approach
adopted by Eric Leyland in his classic Teach Yourself
text, *Budgerigars for Pleasure and Profit*, 1954).
The science and art of history are explored in a
subsequent chapter, as is the detailed relationship
of history to culture. The book was never anything
other than passionate, personal, and committed. Yet
in the chapter "History and Education" it is clear he
is writing in times very different from our own:

It is wonderful how Shakespeare can always
hold the interest of a class of schoolboys. I well

remember my militant, mutinous dislike of Spenser's "Faerie Queen". But not one of us disliked Shakespeare, or did not enjoy reading his plays in class; and, as has often been observed, by the most eminent of scholars as well as by the most refractory of schoolboys, there is a great deal of English history to be learned from Shakespeare's plays.

The early books in the history series included such titles as *Teach Yourself Botha, Smuts and South Africa*, *Chatham and the British Empire*, *Cook and the Opening of the Pacific* (all 1946). By the time Machiavelli and Renaissance Italy appeared in 1961, the series boasted over forty-four titles from *Agricola and Roman Britain* to *Gladstone and Liberalism* and constituted, as had been the original aim, a substantial library of historical reference. Although, as Dr Rowse says in the concluding chapter of his introductory volume:

> You might think that in order to learn history you need a library of books to begin with. But not at all: that only comes at the end. What you need at the beginning is a pair of stout walking shoes, a pencil, and a notebook.

Even so, with a 1946 cover price of four shillings and sixpence (approximately £5.84 in today's prices), it was not going to break the bank to include in your rucksack a Teach Yourself history book along with your sandwiches and a Thermos flask.

CHAPTER III

WORK, REST AND PLAY

1950s

In 1950, as part of the "Teach Yourself
Mechanical Engineering" series, a fascinating
book appeared on the shelves. It went by the
name of *Teach Yourself Hand Tools; Descriptions
and Uses* (Volume One) and was written by A. E.
Peatfield, A.M I. Mech. E., A.M.I. Struct. E. At the
time, along with other books in the series, it was
aimed at engineering apprentices, "mechanically
minded laymen" and "student beginners", and
introduced to them the variety of tools they might
meet in their workshops of the present and future.

The layman reading this today is introduced not so much to a vanished world as to a world running in parallel to the one with which they are generally familiar. As he (undoubtedly a "he") is introduced to the podger, the Tommy bar, the Jenny (or "odd-legs"), the King Dick spanner, and the Dolly (or "cup-tool"), he could be gazing at the hieroglyphics on the walls of an ancient Egyptian royal tomb. What do these strange symbols and objects denote? What arcane purposes did this mute language once serve?

And yet, as we read on, these esoteric pictograms slowly give up a few of their secrets. The shaft or handle of the "hand hammer", for instance, has a "cleft" or "slot" at its thin end. This end is pushed through the whole of the "head" (the heavy metal bit, to you and me) and a steel wedge is driven into the cleft. Thus, by virtue of the extra pressure on both sides of the cleft, any tendency for the head to "fly off the handle" is avoided. And, abracadabra, an interesting etymological discovery comes to light.

Similarly we learn that the "cold" chisel is used to cut away or "chip off" small pieces of metal. And we deduce that any smaller piece cut away from the larger lump might well be a "chip off the old block".

Fascinating. Yet the secrets these strange implements reveal can only ever be partial for, like the Pharaohs' slaves of ancient times, the men who once wielded them are long gone. And this is where the Teach Yourself mechanical engineering library comes in. These comprehensive volumes make up a latter-day Rosetta Stone which, through careful cross-referencing, will enable us to make sense of our mysterious past.

Hand Tools; Descriptions and Uses could be seen as a metaphor for the Teach Yourself project as a whole. Just as the book opened up a new and hitherto closed world to the uninitiated so, too, would Teach Yourself open up endless possibilities for the enthusiast at large.

EMPLOYMENT EXCHANGE

The Teach Yourself series had always catered for those interested in following the traditional trades within building, engineering and the farming industry. As the 1940s drew to a close, however, the range of trades embraced by Teach Yourself was expanding. *Teach Yourself Commercial Art* (1949) and *Teach Yourself Advertising and Publicity* (1950) were among the first to open up new employment possibilities.

The would-be commercial artist – if he or she has hopes of being a Botticelli or a Vermeer – is told at the start to expect disappointment. The purpose of the trade is for artists to sell goods and services, not themselves. After a thorough introduction to layout, lettering, figure drawing, colour, drapery and "glamour" girls, the student is told to get all the experience he or she can:

> Most of you, I am sure, are well aware that merely reading a book of commercial art or any branch of it is not enough. The possession

of a set of carpenter's tools will not make you into a first-class carpenter, and the knowledge of how to succeed in art is useless without hard training.

Teach Yourself Advertising and Publicity (1950) similarly trained the would-be "propagandist" in all the arts and wiles of the advertising world – display, promotion, direct mail, radio, and TV advertising etc. – and was not above a bit of "propaganda" itself. In an unashamed piece of self-promotion masquerading as a "Postscript To The Reader; the next step" the editors pointed out, with not a blush to their cheeks, that:

> You have been reading or looking at one of the Teach Yourself Books published by the English Universities Press, and in so doing, you are one of a good company. Between two and three million Teach Yourself Books have been bought and used and this figure would be many times greater if there had been no paper rationing to restrict their output.

Then, catching the mood of post-war optimism and aspiration, they added:

> The number of men and women who have the urge and the imagination to strive for the full employment of their own lives has never been greater than it is today and they know that the Teach Yourself Books can and do help them to reach that goal.

You had to hand it to them. Shifting between two and three million copies in just over ten years was an astonishing achievement. And mentioning the Teach Yourself brand three times in a few lines shows you partly how they did it. That's advertising for you.

Teach Yourself Freelance Writing (1951) built on much that had been said in *Teach Yourself to Write* (1942) but, in concentrating more on the growing number of magazines and periodicals sprouting here and there after the end of paper rationing, suggested that a profitable career could be a reality for some. Could be.

> No claim is made that before the reader reaches the last page he will be earning several hundred a year by his pen. Success in freelance writing depends on native ability, intelligence and perseverance. But it is possible to smooth the road for the beginner – to suggest ways of surmounting the difficulties and to point out some of the pitfalls.

The book also points out that writing was an area where women could claim equality with men (and, crucially, equal pay) and even, on occasions, surpass them thanks to their "flair for assessing personality, skill in detecting and revealing the 'human angle' and the widespread feminine gift for writing smooth, readable prose". Yet she would achieve nothing, we are told, without the necessary qualities (promoted tirelessly in every Teach Yourself book on the list) of application and solid hard work.

Advice for the budding Charles Dickens

Why do you want to become a writer? Is it because your mind is always crowded with ideas clamouring for expression? Is it because words fascinate you; colourful phrases, scraps of vivid conversation, buzz in your head and shout aloud to be written down on paper? Or perhaps it is that you have something to say, a message to pass on, a gospel to preach, a crusade to proclaim. Or you are attracted by that aura of romance which surrounds the writer.

Teach Yourself Freelance Writing, 1951

Advice for the budding Jane Austen

If she is to succeed, it will be on merit alone. She must learn her trade and win her spurs, play fair and keep faith. The laws of copyright and libel are the same for her as for men, and editors have high standards and long memories which are unlikely to be affected by a pretty face, a pitiful tale or an air of guileless innocence.

Teach Yourself Freelance Writing, 1951

Accuracy, originality and topicality were correctly prized as important parts of a freelance writer's toolkit and anyone reading the book. would have been given a thorough grounding in the gathering of ideas, the choice of an appropriate market, the submission of the finished piece and, before that, the crucial revision and self-editing process:

> During revision, the MS should not be read with the complacent, self-satisfied air of one who says, "By Jove, this is good. All my own work, too!" The attitude should rather be, "This is probably full of error, redundancy, and amateurish faults, some of which I hope to discover before the editor or sub-editor has a chance to."

In 1953, readers were introduced to another career opportunity far removed from the comparatively bohemian worlds of writing, advertising and commercial art. *Teach Yourself Banking* was a solid book on a solid profession written by a solid practitioner who began, somewhat counter-intuitively, "Banking is a subject that should be of interest to all".

Reading it now evokes a world of certainty and security, where the maximum rate of interest on deposit accounts was 2 per cent (until 1951 it had been $1/2$ per cent) and where everyone had an allotted place in the smooth-running scheme of things. This was a time when we had bank managers not financial advisers, when "holes-in-the wall" were the stuff of science fiction, and when the bank took its place with the library as a place of hushed respect:

> Possibly the dignified atmosphere of the banking hall has tended to inspire a certain awe, but the modern branch with its open counter in place of the formal grille or bars, and the personal touch given by the cashiers' name-plates is in keeping with the friendly cheerful, and helpful spirit of present-day banking.

The bank was a place where things rarely went wrong, where new customers were introduced by old and where fraud – God forbid! – was to be avoided by the careful use of personal references:

> It is customary for all business men to satisfy themselves as to the integrity, reputation, and financial standing of intending customers and clients. This is even more necessary in banking. Cheques are dangerous weapons when in the hands of the unscrupulous, who will go to the length of opening a banking account to obtain a supply of them. The general public would not look kindly on a banker who, by the indiscriminate use of cheque-books, enabled such persons to obtain goods and services by means of worthless cheques.

The bank as friend, ally and confidant

To the customer going abroad the banker is indeed a tower of strength. At the head of affairs is the Manager, who, to the customers, is the Bank. They discuss their business, financial, and even personal affairs with him, receive wise guidance, and come to treat him as their guide, counsellor, and friend.

Teach Yourself Banking, 1953

For the author of *Teach Yourself Banking*, J. B. Parker, the bank was a model of stability, a reliable and secure world within which everyone knew his or her place. The hierarchy was immutable and, although junior cashiers could work their way through the ranks to become, in time, managers themselves, the daily demarcations were absolute. At the top of the pyramid was the branch manager:

> The branch Manager has a very special responsibility towards his staff, who look to him for an example of proper standards of appearance, conduct, industry, and loyalty to their Bank. He will foster a spirit of cheerfulness, making the office a happy one, all tackling their jobs with enthusiasm, however routine they may seem. He will take a real interest in his staff, giving praise for good work, guidance on banking problems, and

encouragement in the keeping up of their studies. His interest will extend also to their activities outside the Bank. In short, they will feel they have a friend and adviser to whom they can always turn for assistance. All this can be summed up in the word leadership, which is essential in banking as it is in all walks of life.

The manager's second-in-command was the chief clerk who was responsible for the smooth running of the office, rotas, staff training, and so on:

By leadership and example, fair and consistent treatment, timely words of praise amid encouragement, and the avoidance of favouritism, he will have the good will and confidence of the staff. He will know when to enforce discipline without being dictatorial.

Last but certainly not least (for this is an organisation that relied on everyone playing their complementary roles) came the cashier who, standing at the counter (standing, note) ...

... will normally have more contact with the public than anyone else in the branch. His appearance, bearing, and cheerful, helpful, and courteous manner will do much towards enhancing the good-will and reputation of his branch.

Within this fixed universe, however, there were the first stirrings of change. Although the average age of the new entrant was still seventeen, two factors were gradually altering the profile of the new recruit. The first was National Service, which pushed the entry age up to twenty, and the second, more significant element was the growing availability of higher education. These increased opportunities meant that many of those who would have come into the bank straight from school were now going to university – and causing the banks to ask themselves some questions:

> The problem as to whether university graduates should be accepted into the banking profession, and whether there should be a "two-tier" system for bankmen, as exists in the Civil Service and other professions, has not been decided.

The status of women showed very little sign of changing, where their "opportunities for promotion are definitely limited". Although those in the know admitted they did *not* know the shape of things to come, they nonetheless concluded that "there is, as yet, no evidence that women will ever progress to the highest posts in banking". So there.

All of which was particularly galling, one assumes, for those large numbers of women who had to fill the posts of their (better paid) male colleagues when these had been called up for war service:

> Many, indeed, served as cashiers on Bank counters with conspicuous success. For most of them the return of their male colleagues

from war service called for their reversion to
the more routine, but still very important
duties of day-book or control clerk, remittance
or waste clerk, and ledger machine operator.

That was the statement of the facts. But was it fair?
And would anyone do anything about it? Er,
probably not – at least, not for about twenty years.
Reading all this at a distance of half a century it is
hard to escape the conclusion that, if you were a
woman, the penultimate chapter of *Teach Yourself
Banking* (entitled 'The Way Up') could have been
made up of twelve entirely blank pages – although
doubtless that is not how the "bankmen" of the day
would have seen it. History does not record
whether the consolations of joining the bank's
many sports and social clubs – including "art,
bridge, chess, dance and entertainment, rifle and
revolver, rowing, swimming, and table tennis
clubs; choral, debating, dramatic, golfing, magical,
operatic, orchestral, and philatelic societies" –
were compensation for the limited promotional
opportunities which presumably only the "magical
society" had any power to rectify.

Though Parker wrote of his profession with
commendable honesty (albeit tinted quite often
with a rosy hue) at least one half of the population
would have read his conclusion with irritation and
the growing conviction that, from their point of
view, *Teach Yourself Banking* was, all things
considered, a very good surface on which to rest a
teapot:

The banker must have a wide insight into men and matters generally. He must have a good understanding of human nature, the ability to assess character, and an abundance of patience and tact. These qualities cannot be obtained by studying books; long years of training are needed to produce the perfect banker. Right decisions are often the result of instinct, based on the successful exercise of these qualities; which may account for the often expressed view that banking is an art rather than a science.

Whatever else Parker did, however, he was always careful to underline the vital importance of his chosen profession in not just the economic but also the shared social life of the country. If at times he overplayed that importance and ascribed to banking and "bankmen" exaggerated qualities that owed more to wishful thinking than reality, we could forgive him. After all, he was an enthusiast.

H. A. L. Cockerell was an enthusiast, too, and set out to do for insurance what had been done for banking before him. If it was wishful thinking and hyperbole you were after, then, you need have looked no further than *Teach Yourself Insurance* (1957) and the following ... ahem ... grand claim for his own profession. We begin, naturally enough, with primitive man:

Many discoveries mark long steps forward in the progress of mankind. Such, for example, are the harnessing of fire to man's needs, the

development of printing, and now in very
recent times the application of nuclear fission.
Just as it is hardly possible to conceive of a
modern community without fire or printing, so
it may be claimed that we could not have
reached our present level of civilisation
without insurance.

Putting insurance up there with the discovery of
fire took some nerve, but Cockerell was not one to
hold back as he moved seamlessly from prehistory
to the Middle Ages:

Insurance has brought into our lives a sense of
financial security that medieval man never
conceived.

However, the sense of security that both Parker
and Cockerell described was under threat. Joseph
Stalin may have died four years earlier but his
successor, Nikita Krushchev, was now presiding
over a Communist empire that threatened the
Western world and its freedoms. Moreover, the
advent of Rock 'n' Roll threatened an overthrow of
decency and the values for which the British had
fought a war. How else to explain the writhings of
Bill Haley and the Comets whose "Rock Around the
Clock" had reached number one in the charts in
1954?

In these fast-changing times, youngsters not
attracted to the twin worlds of banking and
insurance now had other options. *Teach Yourself
Grocery for Beginners* (1956) and *Teach Yourself*

Shopkeeping (1958) were amply suited to the task of training youth, as was *Teach Yourself Window Display* (1957) should you have been attracted to a more specific aspect of the retail trade. For the would-be grocer times had certainly changed:

> In more leisurely times a youth entered the trade as an indentured apprentice and served his master as such for from four to seven years, during which period he was taught the "art and mystery" of the trade by the simple process of hard work.

Even in 1956 the book concluded that the "modern youth" would never have dreamt of spending so long as an apprentice, so it had to compress and condense the "art and mystery" of the trade for him – and, just possibly, for her. Cleanliness was, unsurprisingly, the first lesson to learn, and it was vital to have clean surroundings for the display of food that was handled with clean utensils, wrapped in clean paper and served "preferably by people who are clean and attractive in appearance and manner". "Such revolting habits as the moistening of the index finger with saliva to facilitate the opening of biscuit bags" were not to be tolerated.

Care and control of stock were just two of the practical skills the fledgling grocer was expected to master. And there was more. Much, much more. Did he really need to know that the tea-plant (*Camellia sinensis*) required a hot moist area as provided by the monsoon belt of Asia or that tea-gardens were to be found at altitudes up to 7,000 feet above sea level?

Absolutely. Just as he had to know the provenance of coffee and the difference between beans from the "Belgian Congo" and "Abyssinia". It was important to know that cocoa was a product of the conquest of Mexico and that it was in 1526 or thereabouts that Cortes brought the first cocoa beans to Spain. Just as it was vital to have an understanding of all "cereals, pulses, and farinaceous foods" to be the type of well-informed grocer the general public expected on its high streets.

It is, for example, debatable today whether the average supermarket manager knows that the grocery trade owes its origins to the trade in spices or that the pepperers and spicers of old England were the forerunners of the modern grocery trade. Does he or she also know that the Ancient Guild of Pepperers dates back to 1180, or that the crest of the Grocers' Company of London (which itself evolved from the Fraternity of St Anthony) includes the camel and the clove to remind people that the fraternity was once responsible for the purity and genuineness of the spices sold in London? One suspects not. Yet grocers of 1956 needed to have such facts at their fingertips, including a basic grasp of the etymological derivation of their chosen trade. Should you have forgotten:

> The term 'grosser' comes from the medieval Latin *grossarius*, and indicates wholesale dealers in spices and imported produce. To-day the grocer in France is still called *épicier*.

Well, fancy that. Clearly there was certainly more to a grocer's trade in those days than crisps and tinned beans. And a set of revision questions at the end of the book underlined the fact that general and specialist knowledge was expected of all those entering the trade. Nowadays the questions read like starters for ten from "University Challenge".

- Name in proper sequence the processes in the manufacture of tea.

- How is raw cane sugar produced?

- Compare Smyrna, Australian, and Greek sultanas.

- What is meant by hermetically sealed in relation to a can of food?

- What is the ideal sort of pig for curing as bacon?

- Compare total imports of bacon before the war and since the war and the individual sources of supply.

- Name the goods to be sold by net weight.

- What is the legal definition of cheese?

In 1956, Jack Cohen opened his first Tesco store in Malden in Essex and soon the multiple chain stores would be increasing their share of the market. But *Teach Yourself Grocery for Beginners* and, two years later, *Teach Yourself Shopkeeping* (1958) set out to reassure potential and actual shopkeepers that they and their estimated 600,000–700,000 shops in Britain had not yet had their day:

> This textbook will guide retailers how to organise and manage their shops so that they may be in a position to face with good courage and a healthy optimism competition from any quarter.

In promoting small shops over the larger multiples the book was strangely prescient, anticipating the "Small Shops Campaign" over fifty years later. It also entered into the Sunday trading controversy before anyone had thought it an issue and, admittedly in circumstances far different from those today, looked at the pitfalls and opportunities of using "migrant labour" as a way of cutting costs.

The book appeared at a time of increasing prosperity for the people of Britain. Indeed the so-called consumer society as we know it today might be said to have had its origins in the 1950s. A book like *Teach Yourself Shopkeeping* not only spotted the trend but elevated it into a quasi-anthropological principle which it expounded in terms of due awe:

> Mankind spends his money, his substance in satisfying his needs, whether these needs be food, clothing, shelter or recreation. During the past twenty five years in particular there has been an extremely rapid and wide expansion in the needs and desires of

mankind. The rise in the standard of living of the industrial masses has created an extensive demand for goods of every kind. Mankind now desires a higher standard of comfort; greater variety in food, clothing and domestic surroundings all of which have combined to create demand.

Steady on, there. We are surely talking about shopping not the Ascent of Man. Then again …

SEX AND STRAIGHT TALKING

The Teach Yourself series prided itself on exploring new and surprising areas of study, and in 1951 it produced a book that fell into both categories: *Teach Yourself Sex; Its Meaning and Purpose*.

Not that sex was, erm, exactly "new" – although its treatment in a popular, freely available, and extremely high profile series of books such as Teach Yourself undoubtedly was. This was a sensitive undertaking and had to be both clear and frank enough for the general audience while not upsetting the tastes and standards of the day. Leonard Cutts, a devout Christian and, as we know, the brains behind the Teach Yourself project, clearly thought it had succeeded in both its aims when he introduced the book "which can be handed to any adolescent or adult with complete confidence" in suitably sober terms:

This is the guide-book to the meaning and purpose of sex that has long been sought; and no reader will leave its pages without a proper enlightenment or without mental and even spiritual enrichment.

The new book was a far cry from the few books on sex that existed at the time: "most of them were either technical or so strongly academic that they were read only by doctors, nurses, or students". And if any dirty devil were to be caught reading them … or rather:

If perchance they did get into the hands of the unprofessional or general reader, they were cautiously disguised, read secretly, and carefully hidden away in drawers or on top of some high piece of furniture.

While it is easy to smile now at the attitudes of a less liberal era, it is hard to find fault with the author's general conclusion that men and women had consistently sidestepped a mature and open discussion of sex to the detriment of their own (and others') well-being and happiness.

Men and sex; countdown to catastrophe

As an infant, he is harassed by his over-anxious parents if he shows an interest in the genital area; as a child, his questions about the origin of life are resented or pushed aside awkwardly; as an adolescent, he is given a clandestine and veiled knowledge to keep him from fraternising too intimately with the opposite sex. On the eve of his marriage, he is troubled about the physical mysteries which are a part of his new relationship; and after marriage he is frequently either disillusioned by his technical failures to achieve unity with his wife, or he loses confidence in himself because of his impotence.

Teach Yourself Sex; Its Meaning and
Purpose, 1951

The book's aim was to remove the notion of sin from the sexual act and to assert that, in themselves, sexual relations were good, wholesome, healthy and natural. Well, not all sexual relations, to be fair. No, the only acceptable sexual relations were to be had within a heterosexual, lifelong and faithful marriage. From the start it was obvious that a religious worldview underpinned the author's views and, while this worldview was not laid on too thick throughout the text, it became clear by the end that the whole book was essentially predicated on the Christian understanding of the proper purpose of sex. The book was gentle, compassionate and never censorious but it was very much a product of its times and of the prevailing public morality of the day. That the first chapter should be titled "The Nature of the Problem" gives today's reader an idea of what Dr W. E. Sargent's overall approach was likely to be. Chapter II dives straight into the subject with a back-to-basics statement of the facts:

> In human behaviour, just as in animal or even in bird life, there are certain drives which are definitely innate. These are not acquired like a taste for kippers or an interest in jazz music.

Quite. When he broaches the issue of the varying strengths of the sexual drive, Dr Sargent is also careful to keep his comparisons acceptably neutral in character, plumping for a story about how he tried unsuccessfully to mate his young Corgi bitch with a dog that showed very little interest in "the young lady" and which had to be set aside in favour of "another dog of the breed, which because of his exceptional virility had little difficulty in serving her successfully".

Such thoughts soon lead on to a discussion of the expression of sexual instinct in married life. Discarding the language of the Corgi "serving" "the young lady", Dr Sargent now chooses the straightforwardly anatomical penis and vagina and looks at how the sheer hydraulics of sex can determine the emotional quality of married life:

Sexual intercourse is only possible when the male organ is sufficiently extended to penetrate the female sex organ, or vagina, and unless a man feels desire his organ, or penis, will remain inert. His wife, on the other hand, even when not desirous of intercourse, can allow her husband to penetrate her provided she is willing. She will probably admit that the experience is by no means as pleasurable as when she also is eager for intercourse, but since it helps her husband to release the sex tension in himself she is prepared to co-operate as far as she can.

Commendably, Dr Sargent also refers to the clitoris ("solely an organ of voluptuous sensation, and when touched it can produce great excitement") but, in the absence of a drawing, clearly expects the young man to acquire a copy of *Teach Yourself Mapreading* before embarking on the adventure of a lifetime.

Having explained the three ways of dealing with the sex instinct (Expression, Repression and Control) he goes on to quote case histories that illustrate successful ways of channelling the sex drive into other pursuits. Reading them today with our more sexually expressive attitudes there is some unintentional humour to be had, but it should not overshadow the seriousness Dr Sargent brought to the subject. This example concerns a young man "greatly troubled with thoughts of sex":

Had it been possible for him to marry and relieve the tension in the natural way, he would probably have become much better; but since there was no young lady in the offing, and his feelings of guilt prevented him from getting to know any, there was nothing for him – so he thought. The continued living in miserable isolation eventually affected his health, and he was compelled to see his doctor who referred him to me for treatment. I need not go into the details of this, except to say that, being persuaded to give up his routine work for joinery, which is creative in the sense that it is making something out of wood, and to organise a club for some youngsters attached to his church, he soon adjusted his sex life by sublimating, quite unconsciously, the energies. His depression disappeared, and his former robust health returned.

Admittedly, as a case history, it lacks the intellectual subtlety of one of its Freudian counterparts ("take up joinery" being about as useful for fending off sexual frustration as "tie a knot in it"), but it does reveal the doctor's humane and compassionate intentions.

In his chapter "The Deviations from the Normal", Dr Sargent was much more a product of his times. The deviations he had in mind were "masturbation, homosexuality, exhibitionism, sadism, masochism, fetishism, and transvestism" and of them he has this to say:

These perversions, or deviations, cannot be altogether explained by the simple theory of sex repression, because they are symptoms of an unhealthy personality and reveal, a maldevelopment of the sex instinct, but also a psychologically sick person. The sexual pervert cannot be cured by dealing simply with his deviation from the normal, because the sex instinct is so closely interwoven with life as a whole that you cannot trace its abnormal beginnings without searching within the whole mental structure.

Dr Sargent deeply deplored the persecution of homosexuals but could not but disapprove of homosexuality itself:

It was never realised that the practice of homosexuality is a symptom of a form of abnormality beyond the control of those who practise it. But at last efforts are being made to treat the condition as an illness.

And, in an interesting aside, he notes:

I cannot recall any case of a woman who has been brought before the court for the offence of homosexuality; but the fact that they can cover it up, as most do, enables them to perpetuate an abnormality which may influence the sex life of some young adolescent.

While we are disinclined to have restrictions put on our full sexual expression these days and baulk at any moral disapproval of our chosen lifestyles, Dr Sargent was unashamedly judgemental in tone. Still on the subject of deviations, he says:

> The exhibitionist is a pathetic figure, and the sadist is a dreaded monster, but there is another type which belongs to this major group of sex perverts; the pitiful object we call the masochist – the pervert who finds intense sex pleasure in being thrashed and maltreated by others.

However, these "deviations" aside, the author was quick to show sympathy for the trials of adolescence and to offer compassionate understanding to the young man (it is inescapably a book directed at men) in the throes of hormonal forces he does not understand:

> When a boy begins to realise his need for intercourse, and knows that he cannot satisfy it until he is married, he may bring before his mind the image of some woman who has stirred him, but seldom is it one for whom he has respect, because that would produce the feelings of disloyalty to what he regards as good and noble.

Dr Sargent's firm conviction in the fundamental equality of the sexes led him to champion the needs of the woman as much as of the man in sexual relationships, and to this degree he promoted a realistic approach to marriage preparation and a (perhaps) surprisingly tolerant view of divorce. And this from a self-confessed Christian believer:

> I believe in religious or church marriages with all my heart ... however ... the permanence of love does not result from two people making their marriage vows before the altar of God and promising "to love, and to cherish, till death us do part." This is as much an illusion as falling in love at first sight.

It was sound stuff and, if heeded, would have saved countless young couples (then as now) plunging headlong into unwise unions that would end up either in sour and sullen cohabitation or divorce. Even so, Dr Sargent recognised that sexual desire was a powerful means of getting a marriage into orbit. Its closeness and the reciprocal pleasure he took to be both the ideal and the norm played a vital role, particularly in the early stages of a marriage, in forging the links that would bind the couple together for the rest of their married life. While the sexual feelings were dominant in the newly married couple, he wrote, they would "fade out into the more satisfactory and permanent joys of the mind".

HAPPY FAMILIES

At the heart of the Teach Yourself ethos were the traditional values of decency, fair play, hard work and respect. Therefore, it is hardly surprising to note how much importance was placed on that other traditional unit of social life: the family.

Teach Yourself Mothercraft (1950) embodied to perfection the belief that stable two-parent families are at the heart of a healthy society. Written at a time when divorce was a statistical rarity and faith in "traditional family values" was strong, the book painted an arguably rosy picture of the family unit but was no less impressive for all that. We may read its old-fashioned sounding recommendations with a gentle smile today, but buried beneath the idealism and the faintly archaic turns of phrase is a sound book with well-meaning advice:

> A happy baby means a happy mother. A happy mother makes a happy home.

The opening words set the tone completely – with an accompanying line drawing depicting the mother gazing lovingly at her infant while her husband, neat in suit and tie, places a supportive reassuring hand on her shoulder. A Holy Family for the 1950s.

> Children do not ask for riches; worldly goods mean nothing to them. Their primary needs in early life apart from food and clothing, are to be loved, to be conscious of being wanted, to feel secure, and to be allowed to share those things, however simple and however humble, that their fathers and mothers are able to provide.

This is a world of rigid gender demarcations and, within the pages of the Teach Yourself series as a whole, would remain so until the 1970s. While casual assumptions about male and female roles were made routinely, these merely reflected the sexual and social order of the day, where men and women were equal(ish) – if complementary.

In *Teach Yourself Mothercraft,* for example, the author, Sister Mary Martin, may have handed the starring role to the mother, but she was careful to assign to the husband much more than just a walk-on part:

> You will find your husband can be a wonderful moral support to you throughout the whole of your pregnancy if you let him ... I know from experience what a comfort and what a help a good husband can be at this time. I know, too, that no man earns greater gratitude from his wife when she is having a baby than the one who can be depended on to take control in the home.

And, in the era before babies and toddlers had become a mass marketing opportunity, the husband could be relied on to do his bit to save on household expense. Here is advice on how to save "several guineas":

> If your husband is handy with a hammer – and most men are – and you are moderately clever with your needle, you can, between you, make a charming little cot and its stand for your baby.

Yet for all its 1950s homespun wisdom, the book was in many ways ahead of its time noting, for instance, that "bringing up a baby is really a joint concern". And what it avoided was the modern-day trap of elevating a baby to the status of benign tyrant who effectively rules the home and whose every whim must be indulged. Sister Martin was having none of that:

> It is equally good for him [the baby] to find that he is one of the cogs that go to make up the home wheel; not the only cog or, worse, the wheel itself. One of the first things children have to learn is that they must revolve with everybody else round the home circle; not expect the home to begin to revolve around them.

Specimen diet for the pregnant woman

Breakfast: Fresh fruit or baked apple. Kipper or grilled herring. Toast and marmalade with butter. Weak tea.
Dinner: Roast mutton, rabbit or baked liver. Roast potatoes. Greens. Stewed fruit and custard. Water, or orange juice and water to drink.
Tea: Fruit salad. Egg sandwiches. Weak tea.
Supper: Lentil cutlet with vegetables. Fresh or dried fruit. Milk to drink.

Teach Yourself Mothercraft, 1950

"A complete maternity outfit" for the expectant mother

1 mackintosh for wet days
1 dress for maternity wear
1 skirt for maternity wear
2 loosely fitting jumpers (or 1 smock and 1 jumper)
1 coatee (or jersey) for chilly days
2 pairs of comfortable shoes
3 vests
2 or 3 pairs of knickers
2 or 3 petticoats (or 2 or 3 camiknickers)
1 maternity belt
2 uplifting brassieres
2 or 3 nightdresses (or pairs of pyjamas)
1 dressing gown
1 pair of bedroom slippers

Teach Yourself Mothercraft, 1950

Needless expense was to be avoided. There was no suggestion that the expectant mother should go out and buy a whole set of new clothes but rather that she should alter the old. Sister Martin includes handy hints for enlarging a pair of knickers, for example:

One (Fig. 16) shows a sideseam widening, the other (Fig. 17) not so easy to do, has the widening at the front and back seams. New waist bands will be needed in each case. Fig.

18 illustrates an ordinary brassiere and shows you how to convert it into a nursing one. All you have to do is unpick each shoulder strap in front, neaten the ends and then sew on a loop to form a button hole. To the brassiere itself you sew two buttons in their appropriate places.

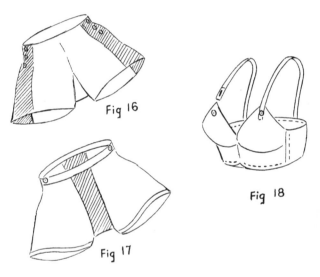

Figure 10 *Teach Yourself Mothercraft*, 1950

And, hey presto, Blue Peter meets Mothercare.

It might have been advisable to preface pages 42 to 46 of *Teach Yourself Mothercraft* with a health warning. Cast your mind back to Dr Sargent's *Sex; Its Meaning and Purpose* for a moment which, you may remember, devoted some time to the adolescent's increasing interest in sexual matters. Remember, too, that this was a far less sexually explicit age than ours today, when the odd illicit "naturist" magazine or an anthropological photograph of naked tribeswomen in Africa were often the only exposure a young lad had to the mysteries of the female form.

Sister Martin's chapter on "Preparation of the Breasts", therefore, with its talk of "well-formed nipples" could just possibly have been of intense interest to the curious adolescent male. What was more, the inclusion of three line drawings depicting the expectant mother's sensuous absorption in the gentle manipulation of her breasts could well have had unsettlingly erotic overtones for some.

A discreet paragraph on "marital relations" in pregnancy is followed by equally important notes on hygiene, recommending that "a comfortably warm bath should be taken frequently, followed by a good rub down and a sprinkle of talcum powder after drying". To those many expectant mothers worrying unnecessarily about washing their hair during pregnancy, Sister Martin offers calm and down to earth reassurance:

> You may do so as often as you wish, and you may visit your hairdresser for cutting, curling and permanent waving in precisely the same way as if you were not pregnant at all.

On the subject of alcohol and nicotine that could affect the baby's growth and heart beat, the author is cautious:

Figure 11 How to regain your figure after the baby's birth.
Teach Yourself Mothercraft, 1950

> This does not mean that occasional smoking is going to be injurious to your child, or that you can never enjoy a glass of wine. But it does mean that if you smoke as a usual thing, you should only smoke now in strict moderation and without inhaling, and also that you are much better without spirits.

The reference to the occasional glass of wine with your cigarette was a giveaway that the book was, if not aimed at a middle-class audience, at least informed by the middle-class mores of the time. The middle class was influential and growing, so it was perhaps only to be expected that it would set a standard by which things were to be judged and to which all could aspire.

The baby's clothing (which only those born long before 1950 will recognise as the "layette") is similarly of a kind that only the better-off could afford. There is, to be fair, a description of "the economical layette" but the general assumption is that little expense is likely to be spared:

> Day gowns can be of voile, muslin, silk, cotton or, for cold weather, nun's veiling.

No, please don't ask ...

> Rayon does not wear very well and nylon is not very suitable because it does not always allow good ventilation. Avoid flannelette. It is highly inflammable and this makes it dangerous.

Figure 12 The Mothering Hour.
Teach Yourself Mothercraft, 1950

Needless to say, the baby would be born into a solid loving home of the kind pictured in an admittedly idealised drawing of the family hearth. A roaring fire (plus sensible fireguard), a toasting fork, and a well-scrubbed older brother playing with his building blocks on the carpet make up the domestic backdrop to mother and child. This, rather touchingly, was "The Mothering Hour" (see Figure 12):

> However busy you are, try to set aside some time, at least, each day, for sole devotion to your little one. Many mothers make this time the hour after tea, when the bulk of the day's work is done and the warmth of a winter fire, or the cool calm of a summer evening are so inviting.

Idealised though the picture may have been, Sister Martin did address the realities of motherhood – from immunisation and teething, to diet and safety in the kitchen. And in a section on contraception after childbirth she also advises safety elsewhere:

> If you desire to space your family it is always much wiser to seek specialised advice on the subject rather than to refrain from intercourse (unless on religious grounds), occupy separate rooms or rely upon the withdrawal method called "being careful" which is not only very trying on to the nerves of both husband and wife – particularly the wife – and by no means always reliable.

Whether dealing with thumb-sucking or head-banging, temper control or masturbation, Sister Martin was nothing if not sensible and understanding. Indeed, it is tempting to think that, at a time when parenting can seem to be in meltdown, an updated version of *Teach Yourself Mothercraft* would be a useful addition to many a family's staple reading matter. Families overstretched by debt and seduced by unreasonable offers of credit would do well to muse on how it might have been if they had been given Sister Martin's advice on money and children:

> From quite a young age it will be good for your child to have a little weekly pocket money. Anything from a penny to sixpence, according to what you can afford, will be quite enough, but the important thing to remember is that he should learn to spend some of it and save the rest. It is a mistake to insist that all goes into his money box. It is meant to be spent wisely and a child must learn this little by little. He must also learn that if he spends thoughtlessly his money will not go far. He must be taught, too, to save up for anything he wants badly. Encourage him to think of others also, and not always to be getting things for himself. Make a point of his giving one or two pennies fairly regularly to charity or other deserving causes, but let it be one he can understand and connected with children if possible.

True, parents these days would be hardly likely to prepare their own "home-made rusks" or rustle up a "bone and vegetable broth" for their infant sons and daughters, but they might just profit from some of the other eminently sensible words of wisdom and advice from a woman who, in her final words of farewell, wants to assist your baby to be "the really lovely child and the strong and healthy future citizen you would, I know, wish him to be".

Teach Yourself Home Nursing, published in the same year, had a similarly settled picture of domestic life. It was not immediately clear whether the book was intended to help the ordinary "housewife" transform herself into a competent nurse if such circumstances arose, or whether it was aimed at the career nurse who would be employed from time to time in a domestic setting. It seems likely, however, judging from the picture of the sensibly clad, no-nonsense female that appears at the start of the book that the latter was the case.

The nurse was told how to cultivate a calming presence, never hurrying or flustering a patient, and always treating visitors with firmness and tact. "Above all be cheerful" was the overarching motto. It was particularly important, the reader was told, to induce sleep in a patient – in ways practical and psychological:

> A warm drink; quiet in a darkened room, a sponge-down if feverish; a blanket-bath or wash; bed-socks for cold feet; a hot-water bottle. And by the way, make sure that the hot-

Figure 13 *Teach Yourself Home Nursing*, 1950

water bottle does not leak, and that it has a
cover. Make no fuss; go quietly about your
work; gentleness, kindliness, a sympathetic
way; these things will help to bring sleep to the
weary mind.

As the text wears on it becomes increasingly clear
that this book was compiled with a grand(ish)
house in mind. It may not have assumed a stately
Edwardian pile or a Jacobean country seat but it
was at least talking about a decent size suburban
semi. The ideal arrangement of the sickroom made
that much clear:

Choose a room facing south or south west; for
in this way your patient will get the sun. The
sickroom should be in a quiet part of the house;
and it is very necessary that both bathroom and
toilet should be easily accessible. A fireplace is
very desirable, both for warmth and for
ventilation: the room should also be fitted with
a gas-ring or a spirit stove, so that food may be
warmed up at any time, and boiling water may
be had without trouble.

The book effortlessly moves from diets and
digestive disorders to the management of
constipation. So far, so predictable. However, the
book deals with one area that would almost
certainly not be covered today outside specialist
nursing literature and is an indication of how far
times have changed. In a final chapter devoted to
"The Last Offices", the author, Mary King Hutton,

deals with the nurse's duties to the deceased in an exemplary and sensitive way:

> When death is approaching, the patient should never be left alone. Even if unconscious, he may regain a momentary consciousness. Probably nothing can be done; but the feeling that someone is near is a comfort, and the patient may want to leave some last message to a dear one.

With characteristic discretion, the final chapter was simply and rather movingly called "Afterwards":

> When breathing has ceased, and the pulse is no longer perceptible, and death is further shown by the dilating of the pupils and the softening of the eyeballs, then the eyelids should be gently closed with small pads of clean cotton wool ... All dentures and jewellery should be removed ... The patient should be left covered with the top sheet, which should be pulled straight up over the face after fastening the lower jaw in a natural position by means of a two-inch bandage tied up over the head ... The finger- and toe-nails must be trimmed and cleaned. The nostrils should be carefully plugged with small pieces of cotton wool ... the other body apertures, rectum and vagina, must be plugged with cotton wool carefully inserted with the forceps ... The hair should be brushed and combed; and in the

> case of a woman with long hair this should be
> plaited on either side and tied with white
> ribbon ... Some people like to put a bunch of
> flowers in the folded hands ... Now cover the
> face with a clean white handkerchief, and
> cover the body with a clean sheet ... Never
> leave any trace of dressings, medicines, or
> nursing requisites in the room ... Lastly see
> that the window is open a little, the curtains
> drawn, and the room perfectly tidy. Then the
> nurse may leave the room, and close the door.

As a model of professional care and personal respect,
and as a glimpse into a solemn ritual that is beyond
the experience and comprehension of most of us
today it is hard to see how those simple, discreet and
non-sensational instructions could be bettered.

CULTIVATING
SELF-ENLIGHTENMENT

"Face the facts of life. Few do. Few dare." With that
stark and uncompromising challenge to the
reader, C. G. L. Du Cann set out to stiffen the
sinews of a nation by persuading people to
confront the truth of themselves and of their
environment in *Teach Yourself to Live* (1955). Or,
as he puts it, to train them in ...

> ... the day to day business of practical living
> here and now in this world, of learning self-
> wisdom and worldly wisdom, of cultivating
> self-development and self-enlightenment.

Here was a man unhindered by self-doubt and uncertainty, a man who held the keys to life and living and who was prepared to hand them over to you for six shillings and sixpence. A bargain if ever there was one.

Control, we soon learned, was what it was all about, the mastery of mind, body and will, which "even the feeblest and flabbiest" could just about muster now and then:

> Feed the will with victories and successes. Do not permit it to taste defeats.

And as for the body, well, "body-capital" was the clue. The more you had of it in the bank, the more you could draw on it at significant moments in life:

> Women, especially younger women, are not in such danger of ignoring the importance of their physical body as men are. They know well the inestimable value of a pretty face, a pleasing expression, a good figure, attractive hands and feet. They know that these are assets and advantages. The youngest, silliest and most flighty often has more sense on this particular point than many clever men.

Still, it was hard cheese on the less attractive:

> Everyone knows that a girl with an ugly face and a squat ungainly figure is handicapped in life.

The History of Womanhood is strewn with examples of girls and women, starting life poor and friendless and making their way to power and fortune with nothing but their beauty to help them.

The key, he believed, was making the most of what talents you had and compensating for what you lacked in physical appearance with good grooming and good manners:

Do not be in the least discouraged if you are of insignificant appearance. Napoleon was of dwarfish stature, so was Lloyd George, and King Richard the Third was a hunchback. Men and women, physically insignificant, can always be of real significance in the world, either by mental attainments, success in their calling, or by attractive and pleasing manners.

Moderation in all things was promoted as the surest guarantee of good health and "vigour". Alcohol, tobacco, even excessive tea and coffee drinking were frowned on by Du Cann who preferred to shun all intoxicants:

The natural drink of all animals – and man is an animal – is pure, clear water at ordinary temperature. Even the iced water beloved of Americans – indeed, all over-hot or over-cold foods and drinks – can be dangerous to teeth and digestion, immoderately indulged in.

From the body and the personality ("what you are") he turns his attention next to property ("what you have"), and warns readers to shun knick-knacks and gee-gaws in favour only of those things that were useful, beautiful, rare or of personal or sentimental value in themselves:

> Against this rule, people say: "But I cannot afford the best." The truth is we can afford nothing else. Avoid the pretentious, the shoddy, and the second-rate.

Du Cann speaks from experience:

> As to the wearing quality and value of good clothes, some concrete examples may speak convincingly ...

> Twelve years ago I had a pair of crocodile shoes hand-made to measure for £10. And worn frequently during that period, they are serviceable and good-looking to-day. "Yes," said their maker, with a sigh, as he inspected them recently. "And if you go on taking good care of them, they'll last you another twenty years or more. The same shoes to-day would cost you £25, hand-made to measure, but you won't want another pair."

Crocodile shoes were only the half of it:

> And I am able to look at my vicuna waistcoat, which cost me a fiver seven years ago, and which would cost £20 to-day, which has been

worn every winter since then and shows no sign of wear. It will probably keep me warm for life, for the tailor of it has a customer who still takes pride in the vicuna overcoat made for him 32 years ago. Such "bests" as these are good enough for life, you must agree.

Du Cann's pithy quotes and pearls of wisdom (on a par with the classics "He who wields the can-opener also carries the can" and "An owl in a sack troubles no man") now seem quite obscure, however, he concludes this book with a line that not only made some sort of sense but summed up the Teach Yourself series in a nutshell:

For it is in living to learn that we best learn to live.

BACK TO THE MAINSTREAM

Teach Yourself the Study of Art (1955) was a typical subject for the period. Even in such an apparently secular field, the author D. Talbot Rice still felt the need to mention, albeit glancingly, the implied religious ethos of many of the books. A comparison between Paul Cezanne and Camille Pissaro, for example, prompted this:

All men, praise God, are not the same, and their visions differ.

Typically, the author displayed the same tendency to whinge over the then state of the country as others had done from time to time. Many of them seemed vaguely ill at ease with the way the mid-twentieth century was turning out and looked back wistfully to a golden age when things were different – and, by implication, better. Rice's final thoughts on art and patronage had a distinctly downbeat tone:

> Perhaps some sort of communal patronage will eventually be forthcoming, as at certain ages in the past. But if so it will be neither Emperor nor Church that has the controlling say, but the government of a welfare state. In ancient Greece the patronage of the democratic city-state produced results of the very highest significance. But it may be questioned whether state patronage in such a society as ours is at present is likely to bring about results of similar excellence.

With so little to cheer about in "such a society as ours" it was hardly likely that Rice had noted (still less applauded) that other great cultural event of the year, the first TV appearance in America of the young Elvis Presley. If he had, one suspects his mood would not have been greatly lifted.

He was gloomy, too, about the direction in which he felt art was moving. It was not that Rice was against modern art per se (although he did note that, while the critics may praise it, the public dislikes it). It was rather that he felt the social and economic circumstances of the day conspired against bringing out the best in a modern-day artist. It would be another forty years before the era of patronage returned in quite the way he would have understood it, but what Rice would have made of the Tracey Emins and Damien Hursts, the twenty-first century Brit-Art beneficiaries, we can only speculate.

Teach Yourself the Law (1955) was similarly a subject of wide interest and in the mainstream of Teach Yourself titles:

> No intelligent citizen should be without this basic knowledge. Not only will it enable him to understand more of what is taking place about him, but it may help him to avoid some of the thorny thickets of the law that await the unwary.

The tone was sometimes arch and self-regarding – "The Bar is the most prodigal of its talents of any profession." "The competition is very great." "Assuming anybody to be so rash as to wish to become a barrister, what does he do?" – but the content was solid if largely pedestrian.

The reader was introduced to constitutional law, torts, contract law, property law, wills and trusts, matrimonial and criminal law and so on, and would have emerged with a solid grounding in a specialist subject. Later on that same year, the reader would have emerged similarly enlightened from close study of *Teach Yourself Practical Concreting*. There was space in the Teach Yourself library for all tastes.

TELEVISION FACTS, FIGURES AND FABLES

Did you know that ...

Her Majesty, Queen Elizabeth II, is a keen viewer when State and other important occasions permit. Her personal television set has a large screen and is housed in an elaborate cabinet providing all-wave radio, an automatic record player, dual loudspeakers and record storage cupboard.

Or that ...

Prince Charles has his own 12-inch table model.

Or even that ...

There are approximately 50 television receivers installed in Buckingham Palace for the use of members of the Royal Household and the staff, with a communal aerial of the Tilted Wire type mounted on the roof. Looking after these sets is part of the duties of the resident electricians.

Well, you would have done if you had the *Teach Yourself Television Viewers' Handbook* to, er, hand. In it you would have learned how to correct picture drift, flashing, fuzzy pictures, mysterious flashes, and reversal of blacks and whites as well as how to assess signal strength from Oxfordshire to the Isle of Wight.

More than that, though, you would have learned how to access a whole new world of adventure, discovery and light entertainment that was opening up to the 1950s viewer. The year before the handbook was published, parliament had voted overwhelmingly to allow the introduction of commercial broadcasting, thereby ending the BBC's monopoly and introducing competition to the airwaves.

The Television Bill was introduced in March 1954 and later that year, on 30 July, it received royal assent and became law. The Independent Television Authority was set up to supervise the TV companies and control advertising, and the first transmission of the London Independent Television (ITV) service began on 22 September 1955. Once again, with perfect timing, the Teach Yourself people had produced the broadcasting handbook for the times.

On the first weekend of the new independent service, Associated Television (ATV) unveiled its legendary variety show, "Sunday Night at the London Palladium", and realised from the off that it had a hit of huge proportions on its hands. It immediately raced to the top of the TV ratings, established itself as the highlight of the week's viewing for millions, and caused at least one Anglican vicar to bring forward his Sunday evening service to allow people to get home in time for the fun. The new television age had arrived and Teach Yourself was there with a guide.

Increased competition was sharpening the quality of programmes and powering innovation in all spheres of the broadcast media. Alongside the variety shows and quizzes, viewers could watch drama and documentaries, have the news brought vividly into the living room, and see the world from the comfort of their own armchairs through nature and travel programmes unimagined only a few years earlier.

Gender equality Part 1

Masculine conception of feminine intelligence may not rank it high in expert handling of television sets, but we do know husbands who confess that they cannot bring the picture to the screen as it should be so leave adjustments to their wives. The feminine section usually furnishes the keenest viewers in the home. Informative and entertaining programmes that provide an afternoon relief to the daily chores when there isn't a man about the house may be the reason. Evidently the BBC realise that the delicate touch of the hand that rocks the cradle is quite capable of ruling the fluorescent screen.

Teach Yourself Television Viewer's Handbook, 1954

Gender equality Part 2

Some husbands lack confidence in their wives. All they expect of them is to polish the cabinet without touching the controls, which are strictly taboo until the master hand of the household switches on.
        Teach Yourself Television Viewer's
                Handbook, 1954

In 1954, the handbook informed us, three and a half million TV licences had been issued. The figure reached five million by 1956 and was set to double again within two years. That meant there were an awful lot of knobs to turn and an awful lot of "master hands" needed to turn them.

"UP, UP AND AWAY ..."

Just as the television (once our husbands had switched it on for us) could take us out of the home and into experiences we could only have dreamt of, so increased opportunities for travel were also opening up new worlds to many people in Britain. Janet Dunbar's *Teach Yourself Travelling Abroad* (1957) was among the first books to tell us how to go about it in practice.

Hers was no mere "guide to picturesque places" but a practical manual full of "hard-core information" (using, incidentally, that particular compound adjective a good sixty years before its time). The first of Dunbar's hard-core facts was cost. Between thirty-five shillings and two pounds per day would have bought a room in a "medium good hotel in most European countries", while between fifteen shillings and a pound would have secured a night's youth hostel accommodation. Camping was the cheapest option which, inclusive of food, would have worked out at fifteen shillings a day.

If you were planning to travel abroad you were expected to put in a bit of effort and preparation beforehand. It wasn't deemed sufficient to stick a pin in a list of package destinations, pack your suncream, and turn up at the check-in. No, as the first chapter made clear, you had to develop the correct "mental approach", which involved rather more than thumbing through glossy brochures while eating chocolates on the sofa:

> Go to the reference-room of a public library, ask to see a large-scale atlas, and study a physical map of Europe. This will show you what different countries have to offer scenically: mountains, lakes, waterways, coastlines. Ask the librarian for the latest Continental timetable, which will also give current fares.

Nothing in the Teach Yourself world was ever achieved without effort and application. The books assumed and relied on the reader's active co-operation in the activity described. Nothing for nothing was the guiding principle. Even something as straightforward as going on your holidays required the same mental outlook.

Dunbar prepared you for what to expect from agency travel but, clearly, as the agency would have been expected to do everything for you anyway, there was a limited amount to say. Far more interesting were her insights into independent travel based on extensive personal experience.

The advantages of travelling by bus in foreign parts

The main purpose of a country bus is to get country people (plus their livestock and garden produce) from one place to another. Peasants are generally constructed on the same principle as their buses; sturdy, impervious to hard knocks, indifferent to appearances. The traveller who elects to criss-cross a country by these buses must be prepared for hard seats, much jolting, and unexpected and unexplained stops in unusual places. He will have neighbours who will take it as a matter of course that he should nurse a brace of wild fowls or a basket of earthy vegetables, and he will have round him a continual stream of chatter, laughter, and song at any time of the day. Country people may be roughly dressed, but they are invariably courteous and friendly, and they will make him one of themselves

> *if he is willing to be friendly in return.*
> *When the bus stops at an inn – which it*
> *will do, often – he will be offered coffee or*
> *a drink as a matter of course; any food,*
> *sweets, fruit or cigarettes which are being*
> *shared inside the bus will be shared with*
> *him too.*
>
> *Teach Yourself Travelling Abroad*, 1957

If Dunbar's experiences were anything to go by, our traveller in 1957 would have gazed on long vanished scenes of rural innocence that you would surely be hard pressed to find anywhere in Europe today:

> He will drive at a comfortable pace along by fields where men and women are working. He will see the children playing and the women washing clothes in the streams, and old men sitting outside inns which have not spruced themselves up to attract the hurrying tourist, but remain tranquil in their faded solidity.

Interesting to note that in the same year that these women were "washing clothes in the streams" in rural simplicity, in urban Liverpool the Cavern Club had just opened and John Lennon had met Paul McCartney for the first time. However, even in 1957, the possibilities for less rustic and more luxurious travel certainly existed for those who had the wherewithal to afford it. What about a cruise, for instance?

> A long voyage is a chance to renew or restore health; many people suffering from overstrain, or recovering from a breakdown, are ordered a sea voyage by their doctor. They invariably benefit, as the invigorating air, together with enforced rest and good food, build up a reserve of nervous energy again.

All very well, but one of the author's two suggested voyages – a 76-day jaunt to Trinidad, Curacao, Panama, Fiji, Wellington, Sydney, Melbourne, Fremantle, Durban, Capetown, Las Palmas and back to Southampton – would have required a pretty substantial outlay. And that was not counting the six shillings for the book. Costs like these presupposed a well-heeled middle class reader, probably on a private income (the kind of reader who would have been drawn to *Teach Yourself to Fly* perhaps) but the less loaded, although still comfortably off, could always dream on.

Back on Planet Reality, Dunbar trained us up in the best ways to sniff out good food at the most reasonable prices:

> A good way of finding out the best inexpensive restaurants is to watch where the workmen and artisans go, in large towns and cities. It is a well-known fact that Continental men are much more particular about their food than are Englishmen, and even when they cannot

afford to pay much, they insist on getting – and do get – the best possible value for their money. I have eaten an omelette in a working-men's cafe which could not have been bettered at the Ritz Hotel; the surroundings would have been more luxurious, but the eggs would not have been fresher or better cooked.

"Getting out of trouble" when things went a little wrong was also an important skill for travellers to teach themselves:

If you have innocently got into trouble, and the equivalent of "I'm very sorry!" does not meet the case, do not resist arrest, should it unfortunately come to that. Produce your passport to the official in charge [and] say "British Consul" in a decisive voice.

Travellers were also encouraged to bear in mind that bureaucracy functioned rather differently abroad than it did over here:

You must always remember the difference between British and Continental officials. They are all bound – invariably – by rules and regulations. But where the Briton is often able to interpret rules in the light of reason, common sense and probabilities, the Continental official acts according to the book because he has had a much more rigorous training.

And, above all, people were told to bear this in mind:

> The one thing you must not do, on any account, is to attempt to "square" the official. Forget all the smart-alec stories about well-greased palms and the sideways wink.

Wherever you roamed, however, there would always be a welcome back home. And the home to which you returned was a stable and, in Teach Yourself terms, unchanging one – even if, Messrs Lennon and McCartney were planning big changes in their own neck of the woods. Testimony to the essentially fixed world the author assumed we all inhabited was her confidence that the addresses of the organisations listed in the book would not change. Would the Co-operative Holidays Association always be headquartered at Birch Heys, Fallowfield, Manchester? Or the International Friendship League at 3 Cromwell Road, London SW7; the Friendship Holidays Association at Beechwood Court, Harrogate; and the Holiday Friendship Service at 48 Dalston Road, London E8? As far as Miss Dunbar could foresee, probably.

If you didn't share the poet Philip Larkin's approach to travel ("I'd quite like to go to China but only so long as I could get back by tea-time."), the Teach Yourself series was well able to open up your mind to the riches on your doorstep. For the reluctant foreign traveller, *Teach Yourself Local History* (1958) was right up his or her street.

Even if you have no qualifications, you will be able to find out how you can in your own small way add to the already existing knowledge of your locality. The housewife on her shopping trips, the schoolboy on one of his prowls and the doctor on his rounds are all busy people. But they are in many ways the best people to promote local studies.

In keeping with Teach Yourself's core principles, the book required commitment from its reader:

This is a book for the enthusiast ... written by a layman for laymen. It is an active book not a passive book. Anyone can attend a lecture on local history, listen to the lecturer and then go home like a two-legged vegetable with no new thoughts and questions.

The author, Francis Celoria, Hon. Secretary of the Hampstead Local History Society, 1955–8, was undoubtedly an enthusiast, and his book was designed for those possessed of an enquiring mind:

"Monkey curiosity" may be our only motive. We are all descended from Pandora as well as from Eve. There is also the satisfaction of hunting facts and solving problems.

The Second World War was not distant history in those days but, for the majority of the population, well within living memory. It was hardly surprising, therefore, that the examples seem dated nowadays:

There is satisfaction in seeing your county
regiment marching in the street past you with
fixed bayonets; one becomes aware of the
battles men of your town have won in
terrifyingly remote parts of the earth. "The
Lancastrians, that's UZ!" said a father to his
little son. A sense of belonging to a place is
deeply satisfying – an interest in local matters
enriches it.

Despite some high-flown language, Celoria had the
common touch and was good at putting the
beginner at ease. For the term "research", which
smacked too much of the Varsity, he much
preferred the words "investigation" or "detective
work", which were much more linked to the
everyday. And besides, he reassured the beginner,
"Some utter nincompoops have obtained research
degrees."

Like many a Teach Yourself author before him
(and quite a few after), Celoria regretted the
gradual homogenisation of the country and, in this
extract, had an interesting observation to make
about London's Soho (whose reputation even in
1958 for sleaze and sex seems entirely to have
passed him by):

The suburban parts of towns and "estates" are
indistinguishable from county to county.
"Mass Communications" are causing us to
have a utility folklore with standardisation of
household chattels, interests, tastes, and
demands. Areas in the immediate periphery of

the centres of cities have lost their personality to big business. An example is Soho, which is losing all its individuality because of the swamping effects of business premises and offices. Soho is no longer a community, despite its picturesque restaurants, shops, and the artificial jollities of Soho Fairs. There is no undertaker's shop in Soho as there was 20 years ago. This may seem a paradoxical way of judging whether a community is alive, but when there are not enough families dwelling in a community to keep an undertaker in business, we can say with assurance that the community is no more.

He refused to part on a downbeat, however, and at the end of the book encouraged the local historian to "do his little bit by trying to make people proud of the place they live in". Then, raising the standard and addressing the troops:

Let him be almost mischievously inquisitive, let him be an adventurer ready for the unexpected.

... he led the charge and was off. You couldn't get more enthusiastic than that.

GREEN AND PLEASANT LAND

The past, as they say, is a foreign country. We did things differently then. We certainly spoke differently.

As and by whom he receives his early tuition,
so will the beginner most probably imitate.
Those entrusted with the task of putting
novices through their paces should therefore
be ... experienced in the laws and traditions of
the game.

Teach Yourself Bowls, 1958

In 1958, a coup in Iraq was spreading nervousness
throughout the Middle East, Fidel Castro's rebels
were attacking Havana, and Russia's Sputnik
satellites I and II were frying up on re-entry into
the earth's atmosphere, but – no matter – the
soundtrack of "South Pacific" had gone to number
one in the pop charts, and all was well on the
swards of Albion where bowls players could
breathe the air of freedom and prosperity while
feeling thoroughly at ease in their own skin:

The warmth and genial outpourings of all that
is best in human nature go out to all players
on the green, the joy of the players is
unrestrained, and the fellowship established
among them is infectious.

In 1958, the people of England had never had it so
good. In fact, they had been told so – officially and
in so many words – a year earlier by none other
than the British Prime Minister, Harold Macmillan,
who reminded them of their growing prosperity
and accelerating living standards. They had paid
holidays and free time. They could enjoy their
increased leisure hours in ways unheard of in

previous generations. They could have parties and entertain. In short, they were lucky bastards who didn't know they were born.

Welcome to the vanished Neverland of post-war Britain as yet untouched by Flower Power and the Beatles, a secure world bounded by the known and the familiar, a prosperous world confidently emerging from beneath the shadow of war. And, as if to mirror those reassuring times, the Teach Yourself series, by now preparing to enter its third decade, painted a seductive picture of the infinite delights and possibilities to be had from embracing one of the myriad civilised leisure pursuits open to all in this era of plenty.

If, for example, the game of bowls were your chosen pastime, who better to consult for guidance and encouragement than James Taylor, Member of Council on the English Bowling Association? How could you resist first acquiring then honing your proficiency courtesy of his aldermanic tutelage? Indeed, how could you resist joining the ranks of these wholesome ambassadors of a game which "except for archery" was confidently declared to be Britain's oldest recreation? In this extract from the introductory chapter you can positively smell the starch and the carbolic, with just a hint of pipe tobacco:

The new recruit to the game of bowls will also be agreeably surprised, and I hope pleased, at the smart attire of the players; all dressed in regulation dress – white trousers, brown shoes with no heels, blue blazers, white felt hat or

white cap with the hatband of the hat bearing
the county's colours. Also each player will be
adorned with his club or county badge on his
blazer.

Surely no finer group of men existed. And women,
of course. A final (short) chapter, "Women
Bowlers", praises their "keen eye for measurement
and distances" and adds:

Women can be just as graceful as men in poise
on the mat and in delivery, and their ideas of
general deportment prevent the jumping about
and the fantastic contortions sometimes seen
when men are playing.

What could Mr Taylor have meant by "fantastic
contortions", one wonders. Could he have been
referring to early displays of exuberance on the
green? Was he describing (and, more than likely,
lamenting) the growing trend towards a particular
brand of emotional incontinence which would
reach maturity in the unrestrained antics of our fin
de siècle football stars? Quite possibly, since this
was written at a time when victory and defeat were
to be greeted alike, with manly restraint and the
firm handshake of the true Olympian. No
punching the air in those days, to be sure, or – the
horror, the horror – no hugging of one's team
mate in a gesture that would be deemed as "sissy"
as it was, well, quite frankly, downright
embarrassing. There was, you see, a proper way to
behave and this wasn't it. It wasn't cricket and it
certainly wasn't bowls.

Figure 14 *Teach Yourself Bowls*, 1958
Reproduced with kind permission from the Southampton (Old) Bowling Green.

DOING IT BY THE BOOK

To discover the right way of doing things you had only to consult the appropriate book. *Teach Yourself Etiquette and Good Manners: A Modern Social Guide* (1958) was just such a book.

Planning to fire off a letter to a duke, a duchess, an earl, a baronet, the wife of a baronet, the wife of a knight, a bishop or a canon? Then reach for your social guide and follow the rules. Specimen letters gave you the correct forms of address and everything else you needed to know to correspond with every class in society. Take this correspondence between "Arthur Willoughby" and "Lady Lavenham":

Dear Lady Lavenham,

When I had the pleasure of talking with you at the Dersingham's last week, you mentioned Sartre's new play, now running at the Thespian, and said that you would like to read it. On making enquiries I was confirmed in my belief that the text of the play has not yet been published over here. As it happens, I saw it in Paris last year and I find I still have a copy of the French edition.

Nothing is more tiresome than having a book foisted on one, but if you would really like to read this play, I will gladly let you have my copy. In that case perhaps you would allow me to bring it round to you.

I remain, Dear Lady Lavenham,

Yours sincerely.

Arthur Willoughby.

Or this from "J. H. Huntley" to "Professor Tweed":

Dear Professor Tweed,

You will probably not remember me, but in my undergraduate days now – alas ! – a good many years ago, I used to attend your lectures.

In last Sunday's *Standard* I chanced to see your letter in which you stated that you were working on a biography of Mendelssohn.

My grandfather, who was a keen amateur musician, corresponded with Mendelssohn and, I believe, met him several times. I am vague about the details, but I still have a kind of scrap-book containing one or two letters from Mendelssohn and a number of press cuttings relating to performance of his works in London. They are of no great interest to me, but in the hope that they may be to you, I am sending the book to you by registered post.

Yours very truly,

J. H. Huntley (St Bede's 1928–31)

Or what about a spot of friendly joshing from "Gordon" to "Captain J. A. Dawkins"?

(c/o The Nomads' Club, SW3.)

Dear Dawker,

At your urgent request I was misguided enough to lend you my cherished copy of Dodge's *Fly Fishing*, which has been my stand-by for years. I ought to have known better. As if there aren't enough gaps on my shelves already to remind me that it is fatal to lend books to otherwise tolerably honest friends! You've had it for at least six months and I haven't the foggiest idea where you are. Probably bagging the largest salmon in Norway, which you'd never be able to do without my book. So send it back before I have the law on you!

My love to Muriel, and all the best to you, though you don't deserve it!

Yours ever,

Gordon.

What wags! My, how they must have laughed.

The behaviour to be adopted when attending a public dinner is probably less dated, since the procedure surrounding formal events at which captains of industry, gurus of business, and big-wigs of all shapes and sizes are present has itself probably changed little. Spot the anachronism these days, however, in our brave new smokeless world:

When the final course, usually dessert or a savoury, has been cleared away, the Chairman will rise and, silence having been obtained, will propose the loyal toast, the customary formula being: "My Lords, etc. Ladies and Gentlemen, I give you the toast of her Majesty the Queen." Those present then rise and say "The Queen," raise their glasses, drink, and sit down again. Some loyalists add: "God Bless Her", but this, though doubtless unexceptionable, is not strictly correct. After, but not before this, people may smoke. Sometimes the Chairman will give permission himself, sometimes the waiters will, without waiting for any such intimation, begin to hand round cigars and cigarettes.

When even pregnant women were advised not to smoke *too much* during pregnancy (*Teach Yourself Mothercraft*, 1950) and when young women attending a dance were advised to take cigarettes to break the ice (*Teach Yourself Modern Dancing*, 1949), it is quite clear the modern reader is eavesdropping on a smoke-filled world far removed from our own.

Formal occasions aside, it is probably in the area of private behaviour that *Teach Yourself Etiquette and Good Manners* shows its age most clearly. The duties of guests at dinner parties were written in stone. Some, like punctuality, may not have changed much:

If the guests are invited to dine at 8 o'clock, they should do their utmost, despite tardiness of taxis, missing collar studs, laddered stockings and the general cussedness of things, not to be late.

As for other rituals, well, judge for yourself:

> If, on arriving at the house, a man is asked to leave his hat and coat in the hall, while his wife is directed by a servant to some other room, the man should wait until his wife reappears, so that they may both greet their hosts together.

Then:

> Having shaken hands with their host and hostess, the newly arrived couple should shake hands with or bow to others in the room whom they may know.

And dinner hadn't yet begun.

> The man should seek out the lady whom his host informs him he is to take into dinner. If he can (without too much insincerity and fortified by sherry) tell the lady in question how pleased he is by this prospect, he will have begun the evening as a good guest should.

As for conversation at the table:

> It is the man's business to converse mainly with the lady he has taken in, for it is not usually possible to talk across the table to any extent, but he should not neglect the lady on his left. This does not mean, of course, that the lady should not initiate topics of conversation herself.

Not possible to talk across the table? The accompanying pictures made it quite clear that these were parties at suburban homes not at baronial piles with five feet of table space between guests on either side.

Figure 15 *Teach Yourself Etiquette and Good Manners*, 1958 Illustration by Gordon Stowell.

Organising the parking arrangements when holding a party at home

If the parking place is in the street, not in the grounds of the house, it would be well to consult the local police beforehand and perhaps to ask for the services of a constable while the party is in progress. A guest's gratitude to his host is likely to be considerably lessened if, on leaving the house, he is faced with a summons for parking his car in the wrong place.

Teach Yourself Etiquette and Good Manners, 1958

As for securing the services of a police officer to help park your guests' cars, well, what could have been more natural? In the sure and certain expectation of George Dixon rather than Jane Tennyson, the host could then rest assured that not only were the cars being parked with the compliant good cheer of members of Her Majesty's constabulary, but that the evening's proceedings had the tacit imprimatur of the national forces of law and order. Now that's a party.

If entertaining guests for an evening was one thing, then putting them up for the night was quite another. For guests "coming down for a tennis-tournament or a dance, to give a lecture, attend a meeting or preach a sermon" the rigmarole was as elaborate and tortuous as preparing for a sherry party. And then some.

This was, in truth, a strange world – a world in which visiting parsons stayed overnight; where people had been to France to see the latest Sartre play and, when in Paris, had of course popped into the Comédie Française or the Folies Bergère; a world in which women withdrew after dinner and domestic servants padded invisibly around a three-bedroom semi.

On holiday, readers were told how to comport themselves in hotels which sounded as if they had sprung ready made from a Luchino Visconti movie. Take this advice on behaviour to one's fellow guests in a hotel. Never mind that the hotel sounded like the one Dirk Bogarde had booked in *Death in Venice*, the rules were the same whether you were staying in a five-star hotel on the Rialto or a B&B in Ramsgate.

On the morrow of his arrival at a hotel, a newcomer, entering the dining-room, for instance, should be prepared to say: "Good morning", as he takes his place, to guests at adjacent tables, or to make some comment on that safe but inexhaustible topic, the weather, to the person occupied like himself in gloomy contemplation of the barometer in the entrance hall.

From then on, however, there were strict rules as to who could say what to whom:

A man can make a few trivial remarks to a guest of his own sex or pass the time of day with a lady in the lounge of a hotel. At the worst he will lay himself open to the charge of being a bore, and to that only if he prolongs his observations when his neighbour is trying to read the paper. A lady, unaccompanied, may have to be more circumspect since she must not give the impression of trying to scrape an acquaintance with members of the opposite sex.

It is easy to poke fun at what seems now to be fake gentility and bourgeois pretension. Yet perhaps it was not fake at all. Perhaps it was nothing less than a genuine attempt to hold on to standards that seemed to some to be slipping fast. In another section of the book the author noted a "marked change" in our attitudes to each other in public and put it down to "a general lowering in the standards of politeness in the post-war world".

Any attempt to arrest that decline was considered no bad thing and though it has proved futile in many areas of public life, who was to say it wasn't at least worth a try?

IDLE HOURS

With the success of its books on the trades and professions and the popularity of its series on farming and history, Teach Yourself could look back on a publishing venture that had promoted knowledge in its broadest sense. It had been equally at home catering for those toiling in the fields as it had been nurturing intellectual pursuits and the life of the mind. It was time to lighten up.

In the increasingly affluent post-war world, opportunities for sport and recreation were opening up as never before. There was, therefore, a potentially huge market for books that would service the up and coming leisure industry, promoting its many pleasures and satisfactions to a population that simply couldn't wait. Books like *Teach Yourself Sailing* (1947) painted a seductive picture of the pleasures just waiting to be experienced:

> Boat sailing can be a means of relaxation, a lazy pastime, when you glide silently between willowed river banks, or it can be the most exhilarating of sports, as you swoop from crest to crest, the tang of the brine on your lips. The choice is a matter of taste, but in either case you will "get away from it all" more effectually than by any other means.

But as usual, real pleasure came with a price: hard work and application. Oh, and between £40 and £50 for a basic general-purpose dinghy on which to begin:

> The acquisition of self-confidence is more than half the battle in mastering any technique, and it comes easiest when the implements are simple. Mastery follows self-confidence, and in turn makes possible the control of more complex and sensitive mechanism.

Before splashing out on your own craft, however, you were well advised to hire a boat on which to potter about and build up your skills. Nonetheless, the complete novice had to be wary:

> Quite half the sailing boats offered on hire are unreliable crocks. Should a sail tear or a rope break while the boat is on hire the proprietor will say, with an air of reproof: "This boat ain't had fair treatment," and expect compensation.

The safest course of all was to join a sailing club, not the exclusive variety boasting retired servicemen in blue blazers with shiny buttons drinking gin and water as the sun sank below the yardarm, but a small local club "where there is little money in evidence, but a great deal of enthusiasm". This was classic Teach Yourself advice.

In 1947 (and for a good twenty years thereafter), Teach Yourself books were the product of a communal world. It was a world of clubs and societies, of public lectures and lending libraries, of local groups and national organisations catering for the educational, social and leisure needs of a population which in the early days was hungry for new ideas and opportunities. It was taken for granted that a club or society of some description existed in every locality and would welcome the beginner with arms wide open into a fraternity of like-minded enthusiasts. Sailing was no different.

Nor was chess. The local club was expected to be linked up with a regional club and could therefore train the beginner to a fair degree of proficiency, entering him or her (though usually in those days him) into regional and national tournaments. *Teach Yourself Chess* (1948) shared the same philosophy as that of the sailing book but, as befitted this more cerebral pursuit, introduced itself in rather grander, more pompous terms:

> The philosopher Mendelssohn gave up Chess because he found it too serious to be a game and not serious enough to be an occupation. If, in disregard of that great example, the reader desires to immerse his mind in this scientific Lido, then the author undertakes in these pages to prevent him from drowning, and so to exercise him that his general mentality will be strengthened rather than weakened by his new pursuit.

In other words, it was a book for beginners. It was also a book for experienced players – but he didn't say that, preferring instead:

And in these pages swimming lessons are also available to those who have long disported themselves in the water.

Oh, do get on with it, man. But patience, patience. These were different times with different standards and higher expectations. And even less cerebral pursuits than chess had their own high-flown enthusiasts and tutors. Professor Ted E. Levey, for example, was "for many years Adjudicator of the British Amateur and, Professional Dancing Championships and Secretary of the Anglo-Dominion Association of Teachers of Dancing", and, in his foreword to *Teach Yourself Modern Dancing* (1949), writes:

> Dancing is a wonderful exercise, inducing mental relaxation, banishing cares and repressions. To the lonely it is the open-sesame to new friendships. My long association with the dancing profession has convinced me that in everyone there is an instinctive urge to dance, and the author, who shows in such a clear way how the first steps of modern dancing can be learned at home, has, in my opinion, rendered a service of great value to the community.

We begin at the beginning, which of course means "many thousands of years back, to the time when man lived in caves and hunted the wild beast for his daily sustenance". If the reader had been wondering what all this had to do with the waltz and the fandango, all would soon be revealed:

Our primitive man, gesticulating with his arms, found he could convey ideas and emotions. For emphasis he would repeat each movement many times, and his legs and body would also be brought into play. Other primitives, watching, became familiar with the movements and joined in the routine. And so, from the rhythmical repetition of these gestures, the first crude dances were born.

Fast forward a mere 20,000 years and it was a comparatively short step, or a Quickstep, to the Hammersmith Palais. The author, Bernard Stetson, presented the reader with a commendably broad and brisk history of the dance before moving on to the book's core and raison d'être: the "ABC of Dancing" and mastery of the dances themselves. He had confidence in his readers and confidence in his own powers as a teacher. What followed would be simplicity itself:

Say to yourself: "There is nothing difficult to learn. Dancing is easy."

And remember,

IF YOU CAN WALK ... YOU CAN DANCE!

It may surprise the reader to learn that people with artificial limbs have taken up dancing and reached quite a high standard.

In short, there was nothing stopping the beginner from taking to the dance floor after an appropriate period of practice, and grasping all the social opportunities that would suddenly be opening to them. It was advisable first, however, to learn the etiquette of the dance room:

> When presenting one lady to another, the younger woman must be introduced to the elder; an unmarried lady to one who is married. "Mrs. Jones, may I present Miss Jackson?" is an example. On introduction men usually shake hands with each other, but if a man is introduced to a lady he must not expect to shake hands unless the lady makes the first move.

And that was just the start of it. For men:

> If you are taking your own partner to a dance, arrive punctually at your meeting place. In the event of the girl being late, it is good manners not to comment on the fact. At the dance, wait in the lobby for your partner. You have only to remove your coat, whereas the girl has to give her appearance some attention. It would be very thoughtless of you to enter the dance-room and then expect her to follow you alone when ready.

And it was thoughtless to ask a girl to dance when she was smoking:

> Smoking usually indicates that she prefers to sit down and relax. In any case it is always annoying for her to stub the cigarette.

> ### Advice for girls going to a dance with a chap
>
> *Arriving at the dance, you will probably wish to go to the cloakroom to put the final touches to your make-up, before taking the floor. As a word of advice, it should be remembered that whilst no man likes to be seen with a girl who is anything other than fresh-looking and immaculate, it is both ill-mannered and even embarrassing to keep him waiting in the foyer too long.*
>
>   *Teach Yourself Modern Dancing*, 1949

And a tip for girls that was very much of its time but certainly not of ours:

> Always take cigarettes to a dance if you smoke. To rely on your escort is really not good enough. If you must smoke, do so while seated; it will look more graceful and less masculine.

Just as Bernard Stetson had made grand claims for modern dancing ("dancing springs from within ... it is life itself"), so similar claims would be made that same year for stamps. What was their power to "weave so binding a spell on those who collect and study them"? Step forward Fred J. Melville, "the doyen of philatelic journalists", to explain. His *Teach Yourself Stamp Collecting* described a pursuit "far removed from the artless game of filling up ruled spaces in a printed book". He begins on a homely note:

> The postman's knock or ring is the most familiar and welcome of sounds. There are few homes where it is not heard at least once a day.

Note the use of the phrase "at least" which alone consigns the book to a bygone era. What would Mr Melville have made of the postal service today? The mere thought that modern-day deliveries would have been reduced "at most" to one a day – and this usually after 11 a.m. – would have left a lesser stamp collector seriously unhinged.

In line with Teach Yourself convention, the author sketches in the history of the postage stamp. This time he is able to dispense with Neolithic man and his hunter-gatherer descendants and, instead, limit himself to the nineteenth century as the *terminus a quo* – thus knocking off a good 20,000 years from the story and speeding up the text no end.

The tools Melville recommended were minimal and cheap to acquire, but the pleasure to be had was in inverse proportion to that modest initial outlay:

> Stamp collecting has developed in many directions, cultural, artistic, and technical. It opens a wide outlook on a world in which international affairs have become immensely

important to the understanding of the peoples
as well as their governments.

And yet the approach was personal and engaging
as if he were the club secretary welcoming in the
new recruit and schooling him in the mysteries of
perforation and water marks. It was potentially a
lifetime's study:

A stamp collection is a thing of gradual growth,
and it is a great advantage if it can be preserved
in an album that grows with the collection.

"Use your eyes" was the author's simple motto;
using them to identify different national emblems,
for example, and to distinguish between the
trident of Manchuria, the hammer and sickle of the
Soviet Socialist Republics and the crescent and star
of "several Mohammedan countries". Enthusiasts
were encouraged to use their eyes to spot "piquant
features" such as, on the common Japanese stamps
of 1876–7, "three-fanned steamship propellers in
the spandrels of the 6 sen., screw propellers on the
8 sen., horse-shoe and whip on the 10 sen., and
balloons on the 12 sen." You really had to be an
enthusiast to want to understand what all this
incomprehensible jargon meant. Then, books like
this had been *written* by enthusiasts for precisely
this reason. Moreover, what they said on the cover
was what you got in the text. Good value, all in all,
for six shillings.

Interestingly enough, a story Melville told in
his chapter on errors and misprints was replayed
in a different form nearly sixty years later in today's

Teach Yourself offices on London's Euston Road. As he told it then, it involved an artist commissioned by the authorities in Newfoundland to design a stamp picturing a seal on an ice floe. Being an artist not a zoologist, the chap drew a seal "with forepaws instead of flippers" and was roundly ridiculed for getting obvious matters of seal anatomy wrong. Bad news for the artist but good news for stamp collectors who regularly got excited about such matters and could dine out on the forepaw/flipper debacle for years to come, chuckling conspiratorially over the confusion.

Easy to mock. Yet when the cover of the 2006 Teach Yourself catalogue appeared with a photograph of the lower portion of a goose standing impassively above a golden egg it drew an impassioned complaint from a keen-eyed reader (see Figure 16). The goose in question, he complained, was clearly a non-egg-laying male. Now, lest the word "clearly" has misled you into imagining that the cover was obviously and thereby offensively "anatomically correct" in its depiction of the aforementioned goose, let us hasten to reassure you that it was nothing of the sort. As you can see, it is a simple snapshot of the feathered undercarriage and webbed feet of a goose – any old goose on the face of it but also a goose which the photographer had assumed to be capable, metaphorically at least, of laying a golden egg.

This was far too imprecise for the keen-eyed reader. Egg-laying, whether of the conventional or phantasmagorical variety, was definitely the province of the female. And this, he maintained,

Figure 16 Teach Yourself 2006 catalogue
Photograph © Corbis

was a male. Checks were carried out, experts consulted, and a conclusion reached. He was right. Teach Yourself duly apologised.

This is an indication of the calibre of reader to whom the series is (and as far back as 1938 always was) directed. Readers were nothing if not perfectionists, and mastery of their chosen field could come only with effort and dedication:

> Success in any activity comes from having a well-defined objective, a clear conception of how it is to be achieved, and the courage and resolution to pursue it. A vague desire to succeed is not enough. Hockey is no exception.
>
> *Teach Yourself Hockey*, 1969

Er, hockey? Yes indeed. And golf, too:

> Diligent and intelligent practice is everything;
> it is the best of all instructors; and without it
> there can be no perfection.
>
> *Teach Yourself Golf*, 1950

Likewise cricket:

> Above all, show keenness and enthusiasm; the
> amount of fun and enjoyment you will obtain
> [from fielding] is proportional to the amount
> of eagerness and zest you put into it.
>
> *Teach Yourself Cricket*, 1950

OUTDOOR PURSUITS

It was attitude not equipment that the Teach
Yourself series demanded. And attitude came free
of charge. The books recognised that beginners at
any sport or recreation should avoid acquiring
expensive kit, certainly at the outset – almost as if
there were an inverse relationship between
proficiency and the size of your golf bag. *Teach
Yourself Golf* (1950) says:

> The sensible golfer limits himself to a kit
> which he can comfortably carry. Yet how often
> do we see a "duffer", with more money than
> sense, hacking his way round a course with a
> complete outfit?

In a fashion note in *Teach Yourself Mountain
Climbing* (1958), the author weighed up the pros

and cons of what to wear over the boot to protect ankle and lower calf from getting wet and decided in favour of gaiters:

> Earlier generations have had success with puttees, especially short ones which do not restrict the calf muscles. Nowadays they are seldom used, perhaps because of the "period" look they inevitably bring to the wearer.

Given that "puttees" were standard Second World War issue in the army (to keep the trouser bottoms gathered in and neatly in line with the boot) it was understandable that the modern mountaineer would not have wanted to be seen in such outdated gear. Such minor vanity apart, the author restricted himself to a straightforward description of basic climbing gear which would be within the financial reach of any serious climber.

In 1958, Maurice Wiggin had the same approach to fishing tackle. In *Teach Yourself Fly Fishing* he made it clear from the off that the sport need not require unlimited reserves of cash:

> I have a notion that there is a fairly widespread idea that fly fishing is a costly, exclusive, and somehow socially "right" thing to do; that it takes money and inordinate knowledge and skill. It is the sort of perversion of the truth which arises naturally enough in a highly stratified money-democracy such as England.

Likewise, Fred Brundle in 1959 and his advice on badminton gear. In *Teach Yourself Badminton* he praised the sport not least because it was an inexpensive one to take up:

> You have now provided yourself with a racket, shuttles, and have somewhere to play. What shall you wear? Whatever it is, it should be white. For men, shorts are almost universal wear, although quite a few diehards retain their long flannels for mid-winter wear, especially useful for sitting around in if your hall is inclined to be draughty. These are worn with either a singlet or a tennis shirt and a woollen pullover (still white please); it is useful to have one short-sleeved, and one long, according to the weather.

And then off you went, Fred's matey encouragement shouting at you from the page.

Encouragement for the beginner

Ready now then? Ready for anything? That's the spirit! A good badminton player is always a little aggressive. Let's begin that way, shall we? Remember you can smash the shuttle with all your might and main! It still won't break a window or do anyone a serious injury. So smash it, will you?

Teach Yourself Badminton, 1959

It was customary in the sports books of the period to describe the ideal match, as if to lure the beginner into a seductive world of skill and grace in action. Here we join Eddy Choong and Joe Alston on the badminton court just before the game:

> As the men players belt away at the shuttles and generally try to quieten the butterflies that persist in flying around the stomachs of even the most experienced players, a horde of well-disciplined and knowledgeable officials descends on the court under the generalship of an ex-international player, an official of the Badminton Umpires' Association of England. You will notice as they finish their knocking up, that Choong has a fluent whipped backhand and moves like a cat across the court. Choong has a plan before he goes on court for any game. He is a law student, works his plan out in cold logic, and executes it with speed, stamina, and accuracy. Alston is a fighter (in private life a Los Angeles FBI man) and hopes to match Choong's stamina and blunt his accuracy by maintaining a perfect length.

Teach Yourself Cricket had done the same in 1950, describing an imaginary journey to a Test Match at Lord's and a perfect day's play:

> By the time we are seated and have bought a "card of the match" it is almost 11.30 am, the

umpires are coming out, and a policeman is quietly shooing the last small boy away to the boundary line round the edge of the playing field. Number one [of the opening batsmen] "takes guard" and carefully looks round the ground as the fieldsmen crouch or stride into their positions round him, and we settle ourselves into our seats for the first spell of play until lunch is taken.

Then we follow play throughout the day "until the shadows lengthen and the sun sinks behind the stands, while the seats begin to empty as their occupiers leave for early buses or trains". A perfect day equalled but not bettered by Wiggins' description of an afternoon's fly fishing:

Come with me, now, to some remote and splendid part of the country that hasn't been priced out of everybody's reach save wealthy stockbrokers'. Here we are among the eternal hills, and we'll just light a fire of twigs and brew up before we start fishing. Around these parts you'll see ravens and buzzards, but no human vultures. That river runs as it has run since the crust of the old earth cooled and shrank with magnificent great steamy detonations. No syndicate of superior persons elaborate absurd rules to govern your conduct upon it. You will be guided by your innate sense of what is fit. You will not poach other men's fish and you will not so work, with stout

hawsers, grapnels, sniggles, gaffs, and throw
nets, that no fish escape your greed. No,
indeed; you will fish like a sportsman, giving
the fish a fair chance. For, God save us all, you
have come all this way in order to catch fish,
and catch them you shall.

This was the life, an outdoor life in tune with
nature, free from all the petty restrictions of urban
toil where a man could truly be himself.

Advice to the young angler

*Put up your rod, then, your limber, easy
actioned, honest rod. Anoint those ferrules
with a film of good oil before you put the
rod together – simply by rubbing them in
the hair at the back of your neck. What a
fool you look while you're doing it. Who
cares? There's none here to see but me,
laddie, and I'd far rather watch a man
rubbing a ferrule on the back of his neck
than a man writing in a ledger or using a
telephone or speaking on television.*

Teach Yourself Fly Fishing, 1958

And by the time Wiggins bade us farewell, in his
final chapter entitled typically "You Can Do It!", we
felt we were saying goodbye to a friend and guide:

Good luck to you. Think of me sometimes when you feel that indescribably thrilling tug as a fish takes hold and the rod leaps in your hand.

From the bucolic to the suburban and from the simplicities of rod and line to the technology of the internal combustion engine. All had their place in the Teach Yourself library. Dudley Noble's *Teach Yourself Motoring* (1951) appeared at a time when:

The motor vehicle is essentially a part of everyone's normal life. We have certainly become a road-minded nation, and realise how much our daily lives are influenced by the motor vehicle.

Noble's purpose was simply to explain all that a motorist should know about a car and its use on the "King's Highway". He began by wondering whether good drivers were born or made but gave up enquiring too much by the time the first two paragraphs were out of the way. Certainly there is such a person as a "first-class driver" but ...

To qualify for that enviable appellation, in my opinion, a person must emerge with credit from a number of tests, not every one of which is concerned with the time the car is actually in motion. But the underlying keynote of them all is consideration for others. There are, in other words, two aspects to first-class driving, the technical and the ethical.

Noble tried to cover both areas in a text that sometimes buckled under the weight of its own verbosity. Simple things, such as the proper use of the horn, produced prose that was as opaque as it was, ultimately, unnecessary – as in the following exercise in the art of the blindingly obvious:

> As regards the use of the horn, the driver with road sense, while he does not blow it unnecessarily, or, shall I say, at places where the onus rests on him to be specially prudent, will not fail to use it as a means of signifying his presence on the road at points where that knowledge would be useful to other drivers.

It is a fair bet that most motorists would have agreed with that – if they had understood what he was talking about. Then there was his description of a very early example of road rage (1951 style) – of which he was well and truly guilty. To understand this you need to know that the "trafficator" was an early signalling device which, unlike today's flashing orange light, was an illuminated orange flag or arm that physically popped out of a recess in the side of the car. Noble writes:

> I remember another narrow squeak when a car, restarting at traffic lights, suddenly pulled right across my bows and did, in fact, scrape my wing. I stopped the driver, after a chase, and asked why he had not signalled his intention of turning. He replied that he had

put out his trafficator, and, when I requested him to repeat the process, as I had certainly not seen the arm, he discovered that the arm was stuck in its recess, although the light inside it could be seen glowing when one stood by the side of the car.

"After a chase", Noble? Good God, man, what had got into you? It was a momentary lapse. Elsewhere he was anxious to promote considerate driving at all times and to promote "the fellowship of the road, the same type of camaraderie which once induced a motorist to stop and offer help to a comrade in distress".

The considerate motorist

The essence of good manners is to be considerate of your neighbour, and that unspeakable fellow the roadhog can be just as much of a nuisance (and danger) whether at the wheel of a fiery sports car or a crawling small saloon. The "week-end driver" who ambles along the crown of a busy main road and dares other people to overtake him – if they can – is not thoroughly selfish but a real roadhog into the bargain.

Teach Yourself Motoring, 1951

The one group of individuals who were guaranteed to have been considerate at all times were the cyclists of the 1950s. A more wholesome band of road-users it would have been impossible to meet – if all you had to go on was R. C. Shaw's *Teach Yourself Cycling* (1953), that is.

"Cyclists" had to be distinguished from mere "bike-riders" who had not yet learned "the easy, efficient, effective style of riding that makes all the difference between 'shoving a bike around' and the delightful activity that really deserves to be called 'cycling'".

At a glance, we can see we are back in the company of an enthusiast. Shaw's target was that group of young riders who "nowadays adopt an absurdly exaggerated racing position for normal riding. They do harm to themselves and to the good name of cycling". Without mentioning them by name he clearly had in mind the holier-than-thou, two-wheeled terrorists on the provisional wing of the cycling fraternity who were apparently as common then as now. Presciently, yet again, this looked and sounded uncannily like an early appearance of the lycra lout. Certainly the text belongs to a bygone age when most cyclists *did* actually follow the rules to the letter. In our present era when rules seem optional, this detail on lights has a quaint and antiquated feel:

> If a cyclist has trouble with his lights when he is out riding after dark, he is allowed to go on his way without lights so long as he walks and

wheels his bicycle as near as possible to the left-hand edge of the carriage-way.

Good manners and consideration of others were taken for granted and needed no real elaboration, but the author spent time trying to instil in the rider good "roadmanship" and the acquisition of a sixth, so-called "detective sense" – the ability to see a situation or a problem up ahead before it had actually occurred.

The text was accompanied by delightful line drawings all designed to promote the joys of cycle touring (see Figure 17). It was essential to have the right equipment, and equally so to store it safely and economically. Mr Shaw had lengthy instruction on "luggage-carrying" and used this as an opportunity, glancingly, to separate the wheat from the chaff:

> The butterfly rider who ventures out only when the sun is shining in a blue sky, need not encumber himself with the carrying of a cape or other protection against wet weather. His kit is so small that it does not matter whether he puts it in his pocket.

The clear though unstated subtext being that these jackass amateurs are in a different league from the rest of us and a book such as this, as pearls before swine, is simply wasted on them. The author, however, puts it more discreetly:

The historic Court House
Long Crendon

Figure 17 *Teach Yourself Cycling*, 1953
Illustration by Frank Patterson.
Reproduced with kind permission from the Cyclists' Touring Club.

The more serious rider will always carry on his machine not only the necessary tools and repair outfit, but also a cape, and when he is going out for a whole day's ride he may take with him sandwiches, and perhaps, a thermos flask.

The sandwiches and the thermos flask alone tell today's readers as much as they need to know about that bygone world of simple pleasures, where people proverbially made their own amusement, were never bored, and got hours and hours of enjoyment virtually for free. Cycling was also a pastime open to people of all ages:

At one end of the scale, cycling is a real he-man's sport; at the other it is the ideal recreation for the elderly philosopher who loves to potter around the country lanes. To young and lusty riders it represents the pure delight of physical exertion (and possibly also the boisterous companionship of other young people with the same delight in hard riding). Older cyclists usually have quieter ideas of touring.

However, for both classes of riders the standards of the time were the same – conservative. On the subject of what clothes to take on a touring holiday, for example, Shaw offers these two alternatives:

Some tourists of the more spartan kind, are quite content to wear in the evening, when their riding is done, the same clothes as those in which they did the day's cycling. Others prefer to make a complete change, discarding the shorts and open-necked shirt they wore on the bicycle and replacing them with long trousers and a shirt and collar and tie of a rather more formal kind.

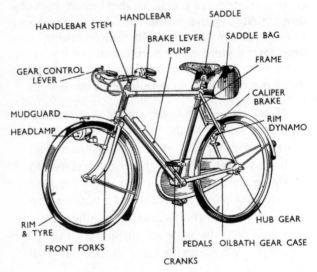

HANDLEBAR STEM
HANDLEBAR
SADDLE
BRAKE LEVER
SADDLE BAG
PUMP
GEAR CONTROL LEVER
FRAME
MUDGUARD
CALIPER BRAKE
HEADLAMP
RIM DYNAMO
RIM & TYRE
HUB GEAR
FRONT FORKS
PEDALS OILBATH GEAR CASE
CRANKS

The Main Parts of a Bicycle

Figure 18 *Teach Yourself Cycling*, 1953
Illustration by Frank Patterson.
Reproduced with kind permission from the Cyclists' Touring Club.

This was, in short, an innocent world of innocent pleasures and wholesome companionship to be found, at their best, in the cycling club. On the road, the cycling club ensured that group riding was carried out safely and with due consideration to others. It appointed a "captain" at the front and a "second in command" at the rear to marshal its riders and give the signal (with a shout) to pull over and stop. But times were changing – even then:

> In the old days, when cycling-club members all wore uniforms, whistles or bugles were used for this purpose, but nowadays the almost universal practice is for the captain to control his party by word of mouth. What we may have lost in pageantry and military precision we have undoubtedly gained in simplicity and clarity.

With or without uniforms, whistles or bugles, the clubs were the guarantors of only the highest standards:

> Clubs are usually very proud of their reputation and do everything they can to enhance the good name of cyclists as a whole. In fact, the most severe critics of cycling "yobs" are the cycling clubs.

The camaraderie of the clubhouse

In winter all the popular cycling clubs organise indoor attractions, and most of them have regular clubroom meetings. There members assemble for games, competitions, lantern lectures, film shows, dances and so on. Whist drives, beetle drives and other card contests are naturally popular, as are table tennis, draughts, dominoes and – just ordinary plain chin-wagging, chatting among old cronies, recalling past rides and planning others for the future.

Teach Yourself Cycling, 1953

In a world of gang "culture", predatory hoodies, and many youths deprived of all aspiration, there may be a lot to be said for beetle drives, draughts and lantern lectures. Yet somehow one imagines few will turn to *Teach Yourself Cycling* to revive them. Those simpler, more innocent times have gone for good.

The following year saw the welcome return of Dudley Noble whom we last met giving chase to a chancer who had "cut across his bows" at the lights. He returned, in tandem with A. J. Shimmin, to produce *Teach Yourself Motor Boating* (1954).

Clearly a life-long lover of things motorised, Noble tried to put his finger on what were the essential attractions of the hobby. It was partly due to its being a pastime that could be enjoyed by "young and old, rich and not-so-rich [aka rich and not-so-poor], by women as well as their menfolk". The cabin cruiser was also a great place to instil self-reliance in children and allow people to enjoy "the infinite variety of scenery, the healthy, open-air life, the wonderful feeling of independence". Although there was something else at the root of motor-boating's undoubted allure:

> The thrill of command, the unselfish comradeship of all who love "messing about in boats" – all contribute to the joy of motor boating.

As if to underline motor boating's evident pleasures, the book's cover photograph was of two weekend sailors, in blazers and ties, both puffing earnestly on pipes and clearly savouring the thrill of command while their "womenfolk" were mysteriously absent (see Figure 19). Were these unnamed sailors early prototypes for Sandy and Julian on the BBC Home Service's popular "Round the Horne" or were they perhaps Noble and Shimmin themselves, their lady wives below deck, preparing a snack for their beloved matelots magisterially at the helm? Alas, we shall never know.

Figure 19 *Teach Yourself Motor Boating,* 1954
Photograph © IPC+ Syndication

INDOOR FUN

Away from the fresh air and the waves, the master model maker H. S. Coleman turned his attention to indoor pursuits and to the "Why, when, where, and how of a recreation which is bringing happiness and a wonderful new interest to tens of thousands". *Teach Yourself Modelcraft* (1952) was in business.

First the model maker needed to find a suitable place to work, not necessarily a workshop but "some reasonably commodious room in which to operate". After that he had all the time in the world to devote to his craft:

The poet is now told how many lines he may
write; the broadcaster how long he may talk.
The journalist must supply "pep" to the public
as a condition ranking before truth. The
carpenter sells his time and skill by the
jealously guarded hour. But the model maker
does his work because he loves it.

Nevertheless, the claims Coleman made for his
craft went far beyond the commonplace. What was
just plain, well, *model making* to most people was
imbued with a social, almost spiritual dimension
that had the capacity to change people's lives:

There is, within the mixed fraternity of model-
workers, a common interest which, bringing
all manner of people together, does for them a
great and significant work. Modelcraft makes
for humanitarianism.

Crikey. And you thought it was just balsa wood and
matchsticks. No, far from it. This was nothing short
of a panacea:

In these days of restrictions it is good for us to
have our minds set free in the realm of a new
interest. If our authorities really knew the
value of such a recreation, revealing itself in
its capacity to keep people contented in days of
endemic discontent, they would no doubt
considerably extend their generosity towards
the home handicraft, and would do more than
they do at present to encourage it.

Yet perhaps "our authorities" *did* know something about the hobby's capacity for promoting social contentment. We learn from Coleman, for example, that during the recent war, when not doing something such as merely fighting the Nazis, officials found time to set up a vital service for the British people – the British Railway Modelling Standards Bureau, no less. This presumably monitored the nation's morale and, if it showed any signs of dipping, immediately dispatched a crack squad of o-gauge modellers to restore peace of mind.

Moreover, officials from the Bureau would have been immediately recognisable because model makers, in Coleman's book, were a breed apart. Outwardly no different from their fellow men, they were, nonetheless, very special creatures beneath the skin, and their interior life burnt with a restless energy and a compulsion to observe and recreate. Take two men on a train:

> One of them is simply "going somewhere", and is infinitely bored by the journey. He reads his newspaper, he yawns, takes a smoke, disposes himself to sleep. The other man happens to be interested in railway modelling or in period architecture from the same standpoint. To him, the whole journey is an education and a wide-awake feast. He gazes out of the window and misses nothing. In his fascination with the things he sees he may even be neglectful of his associates en route. Every gutter of every house-roof, every style of window-frame, each

gable shape, each signal cabin, station sign, platform barrow and advertisement has significance and interest for him.

Far from being a "decrepit indoors man who cannot indulge in healthier outdoor pursuits", the modeller is, on the contrary, seething with life and insatiable curiosity, enjoying "the delights of the occasional club meeting, the international correspondence to which it leads, the companionable interest which can be shared by man and wife or father and son".

Attention to detail was everything and the book spared us none. A yard length of railway track could be knocked up in a fortnight by a mere dabbler, but the true devotee could spend two years on the same thing. How? Read and learn:

There will be the correct laying and ballasting of the tracks, the arrangement of the drainage conduits on each side, the grading of the road-bed, the super-elevation of the curves, the colouring of the rail, chairs and sleepers, the making, spacing and fitting of telegraph poles and signals, the guying of the poles when fixed, the question of lighting installation, the surfacing of any embankments or cuttings that occur, the presence or absence of point-rodding, signal cables, ramps, fencing, and so forth. And we have not yet even approached the matter of buildings with their important details.

Strangely, we never learned whether model makers had girlfriends.

For animal lovers, 1954 was a bumper year. Two new Teach Yourself titles appeared: *Teach Yourself Indoor Aquaria* and the seminal *Teach Yourself Budgerigars for Pleasure and Profit*. In the first, we are taken back in time to the moment it all began:

> The author, when a small boy, like countless other bent pin and jam-jar tyros, with jars all crammed to the brim, wondered why the results of the chase, generally small Carp, Roach, Stickle-backs, Minnows and Dragon-fly or Water-Beetle larvae never survived longer than a few hours. He and his brother then built a garden fish pond, and a few years later an indoor aquarium.

And from that moment on he was ... well ... hooked. In 180 pages, the author told us everything we needed to know about "the apparently independent world we call an aquarium" and, in fact, rather more than was strictly necessary to lead a full and productive life. However, as usual, the writer was someone who was determined to deal with his subject exhaustively.

Eric Leyland continued in the same vein, this time swapping fins for feathers in his lifelong quest to explain all about "this undoubtedly fascinating bird", the budgie. He was not alone:

The Budgerigar Society has enrolled thousands of members, but these represent only a small proportion of the total number of breeders. Budgerigars have come to stay.

The attraction of this feathered creature was, said Leyland, largely due to its engaging personality:

In individual birds the variety of personality is as wide as in human-beings. Budgerigars get in your blood, there is no doubt about that. The affection felt for them is very akin to that felt for human friends.

And to underline the companionability of these delightful birds, Leyland adds a homely and personal touch:

At this very moment my own pet, Georgie, is sitting on my right hand as I type.

It was a picture of domestic bliss from which all that was probably missing was, again, a girlfriend.

If mockery never seems very far off when looking back through books like this it is because there is a fine line between the enthusiast and the monomaniac, between the keen practitioner and the classic single-issue bore. The Teach Yourself author could at times come very close to appearing not only keen but obsessive about his chosen hobby. Those who did not share a similar passion may have found it odd and occasionally absurd – but Georgie was almost certainly not among them.

It is precisely to the keen and enthusiastic that one turns when setting out to acquire knowledge and, on balance, it is fair to conclude that the Teach Yourself books – passionate, thorough, enthusiastic and committed – come out on the right side of the obsessive and the monomaniacal. Or, to put it another way, no more wisecracks about girlfriends.

From cages and equipment to management of stock, breeding, and the treatment of diseases, Leyland introduced the beginner to every aspect of his chosen hobby. If pleasure was one of the stated benefits of budgie ownership so, too, was profit, and Leyland's advice on book-keeping was invaluable. Breeding, selling, even judging at shows were all potentially lucrative pursuits that could add significantly to the domestic income stream. Not only that. We were confidently informed that the construction of a handsome and eye-catching outdoor aviary would "add greatly to the attraction of any house or garden" – but presumably only if house buyers didn't mind a light dusting of guano a few feet from the French windows.

Leyland's stated intention was "to explain clearly and lucidly the main essentials about keeping and breeding budgerigars". By the end of the book, he could justly consider himself successful.

In their different ways, all the Teach Yourself authors could claim to be "leading authorities" in their chosen fields, though few went to quite the same lengths as W. E. Shewell-Cooper to prove it. To say that his credentials, listed on the title page of *The ABC Guide to Garden Flowers* (1955), were extensive was something of an understatement:

THE ABC GUIDE TO GARDEN FLOWERS

by

W.E. SHEWELL-COOPER

M.B.E., N.D.H., F.L.S., F.R.S.A., F.R.S.L., F.R.H.S., Dip.Hort. (Wye).

Fellow of the Horticultural College, Vienna.

Director, The Horticultural Educational and Advisory Bureau

and, Principal, The Horticultural Training Centre, Thaxted.

Lately H. Superintendent, Swanley Horticultural College.

Sometime Horticultural Advisor to the Warwickshire and Cheshire County Councils.

Sometime garden Editor, B.B.C. North Region.

Command Horticultural Officer, S.E. and eastern Commands 1940–8.

The book came with plaudits culled from the *Fruitgrower*, the *Financial Times* and the *Observer*, in which the distinguished English author and garden enthusiast Vita Sackville-West appeared uncharacteristically lost for words. In the *Observer* review reprinted on the flyleaf she was quoted merely as saying, "The best book on vegetables I have yet seen." – despite there having been no reference to vegetables of any kind in nearly 200 pages of text and illustration. Odd.

TEACH YOURSELF AT TWENTY

In 1958, twenty years after the appearance of the first Teach Yourself book, *A Concise Guide To Teach Yourself* was published as an anniversary tribute to the longevity of the series. Part back catalogue and part appreciation, it contained a foreword from Ritchie Calder, which itself bears the marks of another age. The first sentence lends a patrician air to his musings and sets the tone for what follows:

> I shall always remember a caddie who carried my golf clubs at Gleneagles. He discussed Kant and Hegel and quoted Spinoza. Yet he had left school at thirteen to go down the pit. All his life he had worked at the coalface until, in the years of the depression, he was out of work; and then, for the first time, he had enforced leisure which he could turn into study. And he taught himself philosophy.

By that time there were some 300 titles on the list and sales were numbering "many millions". Hardly surprising, then, that Ritchie Calder had come across the books in the unlikeliest of places:

> In a small town in Scotland, I went into the general store to savour the nostalgia of remembered smells – clove lozenges and

linseed cake, paraffin and molasses, embrocation and new-baked bread. And there on the shelf, jostling a display of tinned pineapple, was a collection of "Teach Yourself" – a promiscuous array, Joad's Philosophy; Plumbing; Fishing; Sex, Its meaning and Purpose; Contemporary Literature; Ethics; Greek. "But who on earth buys Ethics around here?" I asked Old Mac, the storekeeper. "Nane o' y'r superceeliousness," he said, "I selled one last week to Jock that drives the station-waggon. And Greek? The game-keeper's son has got a bursary to St. Andrews and the fayther disna' want the lad to be ashamed o'him."

It was an indication of the extent and reach of the series. What was more, the mere appearance of an anniversary edition looking back and looking forward was proof that the whole Teach Yourself venture had become a publishing phenomenon.

The concise guide was a catalogue (and therefore something of a self-promotional tool), but it had as much to do with celebration as it did with pure advertising. Leonard Cutts himself had no problem with the word "catalogue", as he wrote in the preface:

Imagine yourself in some far island, utterly removed from towns and shops, receiving the mail order catalogue of some large store. At once you are involved in fashions and new gadgets and delectable tinned foods – all the multifariousness of urban and scientific civilisation. You are not likely to buy more than a few of these marvels, but you will get a great deal of pleasure dallying with the idea that you *might*, in knowing that they are there for you.

And that, in brief, had been Cutts' aim from the outset:

So it is with *A Concise Guide to Teach Yourself*. It is not meant just to help you find the book you know you want – though of course it does do that, and every aid in the way of index and cross-reference is given to this end. But far more it is meant to introduce you, as agreeably as possible, to the infinite variety of knowledge, the endless things you could learn, and make, and do if life were only long enough.

By now the range of titles was impressive. The 1958 catalogue lists, among others, *Teach Yourself Amateur Acting*, *Archaeology*, *Astronomy*, *Beekeeping*, *Billiards and Snooker*, *Book-keeping*, *Business Organisation*, *Catering*, *Chemistry*, *Christian Theology*, *Conjuring*, *Dutch*, *English for Swahili-speaking People*, *Forestry*, *French*, *Geography*, *Geometry*, *Handwriting*, *Insurance*, *Italian*, *Japanese*, *Judo*, *Joinery*, *Journalism*, *Latin*, *Local Government*, *Management*, *Meteorology*, *Navigation*, *Norwegian*, *the Organ*, *Perspective Drawing*, *Preaching*, *Quantity Surveying*, *Roofing*,

Rugby Football, *Salesmanship*, *Self-Defence*, *Teaching*, *Travelling Abroad*, *Urdu*, *Window Display*, *Western Thought* and *Yoga* (for "Z" readers would have to wait until 1962 and *Teach Yourself Zen*). And this was not counting the already impressive "Junior Teach Yourself" series which introduced children to the delights of *Ballet* and *Glove Puppetry*, *Riding* and *Radio*, *Sailing* and *Soccer* and lots more.

The 1950s were drawing to a close and an altogether ruder age was about to dawn. The "Swinging Sixties" would not be noticed as such by most people until the decade was almost over, so the transformation from ancient to modern would not be immediate. In many ways the Teach Yourself series highlights the 1950s tension between the old and the new.

The reason for this can be guessed at from a quotation that had appeared much earlier, in the 1943 edition of *Teach Yourself Bee-Keeping*. It was from Alexander Pope and, although it was aimed at the modern bee-keeper who had learned to harness both the best of the old practices and the best of the new, it could have been referring to the Teach Yourself approach as a whole:

Be not the first by whom the new is tried,
Nor yet the last to lay the old aside.

And yet, for all that, the subjects the series covered were very much of the moment and catered for all tastes, high and low, academic and sporting, popular and traditional. Or as Calder put it:

The challenge of our times to the individual citizen is that he has to discover and find time to learn so much about so many things. Nobody really knows what he is missing until he is reminded of it. Purposeful relaxation is always beneficial and rewarding. A certain Hon. Academician-Extraordinary of the Royal Academy contrived to become a painter (and a bricklayer!) in intervals of being a Prime Minister running a war, writing volumes and acquiring the Nobel Laureate for Literature. There is a little bit of Churchill in most people, but they have to discover it for themselves.

CHAPTER IV

MODERN TIMES

1960s

For those who subscribe to the theory that the beating of a butterfly's wings in one continent will contribute inexorably to the forces that produce a tsunami in another, 1960 was an important year. The Quarry Men, a Liverpool band, changed their name to the Silver Beetles and embarked on a nine-day tour of northern Scotland. A few months later they performed in Hamburg under their new name of The Beatles and the rest is fairly well known. However, the chronology is significant only with the benefit of hindsight.

For most people, the "Swinging Sixties" got off to a slow start and it was only as they were drawing to a close that the majority of the population awoke to them. Press and TV produced features on "Swinging London" from time to time, but the country as a whole didn't swing until the decade was nearly out. It was not until 1967 that Radio 1 was launched (filling the market vacated by pirate radio stations such as Radio Caroline and Swinging Radio England) and two years later that the anti-establishment fashion store Biba opened on Kensington High Street in London. It was hardly surprising that Teach Yourself was slow to respond to the changes.

"PEOPLE WITH A PURPOSE"

In 1960, oblivious to the imminent popularity of the "Mersey Sound", *Teach Yourself Speech Training* confidently asserts that:

> The flat almost toneless Liverpool accent is the result of a failure to open the teeth properly.

And adds for good measure:

> The Dublin twang comes from an abnormally high incidence of nose and throat ailments in the poorer quarters of the city.

"Modern" though 1960 undoubtedly was chronologically, it had one foot firmly planted in a past where certainties and absolutes ruled. This was not yet the age of relativism. And in what was considered to be "considerably more than just

another book of elocution", the author stresses
that the title was in the mainstream Teach Yourself
tradition of self-improvement:

> Not being able to express one's thoughts
> adequately is one of life's greatest frustrations.
> It stunts mental development and prejudices
> one's chances of fulfilment in all spheres of
> human activity. This is a practical book for
> people with a purpose.

This was a book as much about form as about
content. How you spoke mattered enormously
and, to get on in life, it was well worth practising
phrases like:

> Harriet had her hand on her handbag.

Going along with the general downward drift of
self-expression was simply not an option. Or to put
it another way:

> Catch-phrases taken from radio and television
> comedy series are the refuge of the witless and
> the standby of those too idle to be original.

Oo, er, missus. It definitely was a time to be
serious. Not least because the author believed the
country was at a watershed:

> Easily acquired luxuries are making us soft.

A stiffening of both upper lip and sinews was
required if we were all, individually and
corporately, to make our mark on history.

Going for it

The timid person who is content with daydreams of realization savours neither the salutary effect of failures nor the satisfaction of successes. Action is the keynote.

Teach Yourself Speech Training, 1960

It was easy to forget that the subject that had prompted such thoughts was "merely" speech training. Nonetheless, in Teach Yourself thinking, there was nothing that was "merely" anything. All knowledge was valuable both in itself and as part of a greater whole. Life was for learning and we would be foolish to sleepwalk through it. In other words, we should pick up a book and teach ourselves something. Anything. From aquaria to Zen.

HEARTH AND HOME

From the very start of the series in 1938, the family had occupied a special place in the Teach Yourself series. Idealised and even sentimentalised at times, it was viewed as the core unit of a healthy and well-functioning society. Although the series promoted academic subjects and always fostered the life of the mind, although it encouraged the acquisition of professional skills and practical trades, although it catered for sports and other leisure pursuits, it was to the home that the series always returned.

The home could be school and university rolled into one. It could be the place in which to take up an all-consuming hobby or master a foreign language. It was the place where you could lay down a cellar full of clarets and Burgundies (*Teach Yourself Wine*, 1968), start a collection of English oak furniture (*Teach Yourself Antique Collecting*, 1963), appreciate the intricacies of Japanese paper folding (*Teach Yourself Origami*, 1968), or follow the historical development of English fashion (*Teach Yourself English Costume Through the Ages*, 1966).

Of course, laying down a cellar full of Burgundies in a council house in Bracknell or building up a fine collection of English misericords in a high rise in Bermondsey was probably not going to happen in practice. Yet the possibility was there in principle.

Until even the late 1970s, the home, as portrayed by Teach Yourself, was strangely fixed in time. It had a permanently old-fashioned 1950s feel to it, as if moored to a notional golden age of security and solidity. If one book illustrates the phenomenon to perfection, it is *Teach Yourself Children's Tailoring* (1960). Conservative in outlook, underpinned, as ever, by the twin principles of thrift and self-reliance, the book aimed to give the lie to the common fallacy that "home-made coats do not look smart". This was a gross slur on home seamstresses everywhere (and it was broadly assumed that *every* woman was – or could be – a genius with needle and thread). *Children's Tailoring*, however, took her native skills to a new level, explaining how to make up boys' shirts and girls' blouses, blazers, double-breasted jackets, shorts, trousers and even duffel coats. What was more, it heroically assumed children would want to *wear* them beyond the age of five.

Within a mere seven years, rumours would be reaching these shores of a "Summer of Love"; hippies would be wearing tie-dye T-shirts, bell-bottom trousers and flowers in their hair. For now, though, young women were encouraged to hone their skills binding button-holes and knocking up Raglan coats. In America, Elvis Presley was being discharged from the army while in Britain, the farthing ceased to be legal tender and the country's first national soap made its TV debut in the form of "Coronation Street".

If the times were a-changing, news had not yet reached the home front, where women were beavering away producing velveteen-covered buttons, coloured piping and scallop trimmings, stitching boys' caps, girls' bonnets and generally churning out Peter Pan collars and belted overcoats as if there were no tomorrow.

Teach Yourself Budgeting and Home Management (1964) seemed similarly marooned in a 1950s time warp. The advice it gave, however, was of enormous value, especially to young newly-weds setting up home without any formal training in financial management. Tips on household economies have become the staple of women's magazines and newspaper weekend supplements, but in 1964 those interested in making home

economies could find all the information available
between two covers for the price of seven shillings
and sixpence:

> Don't be discouraged if your united resources
> come nowhere near obtaining the "home of
> your dreams". But try to have a mental picture
> of what you are aiming at so that every choice,
> every purchase and every gift will contribute to
> your ultimate goal.

It was taken for granted that the newly married
couple (or the "bachelor man or woman") would
have put every effort into saving money for their
first home, whether they intended buying or
renting. Financial prudence was recommended at
all times and it was unthinkable that men and
women would stretch themselves beyond what
they knew they had in the bank. Apart from the
mortgage, the notion of credit was entirely absent
from Teach Yourself thinking. Accommodation
settled, it was time to "turn next to the important
job of planning furniture and equipment":

> A good way to start is to make a plan of each
> room in your house or flat. Use sheets of
> squared paper, taking one square to a foot,
> enter the measurements of the walls, and
> mark in all the doors, windows, alcoves, fitted
> cupboards or shelves, electric points, etc. A
> plan of this kind will be invaluable when you
> are shopping for furniture and fittings.

Today's modern couple stepping into a store to arrange for a kitchen to be fitted will be given the self same advice as that from over forty years ago. The only difference will be that the washing machine, the granite work surface, the swing-out larder, the butler's sink, the built-in dishwasher, and the eye-level cooker will be bought there and then – while the 1964 couple would have been contemplating saving for a couple of years just to be able to afford one item.

Read and weep

A "bed-sitter" with gas fire and ring may cost up to £4 10s. a week, (to rent) and furnished flats anything from £6 to £20 a week. In outer London and other towns, a three-roomed flat, with kitchen and bath, may cost £6 6s. to £10 10s. a week; in small towns and country districts prices may be lower.
Teach Yourself Budgeting and Home Management, 1964

Those who are bursting blood vessels to try and pay the mortgage repayments today should perhaps avoid page 47 on conveyancing costs. In the left-hand column under "Price of Property" such bizarre figures as these appear: £1,000; £2,000; £2,500; rising to a colossal £4,000. Yes, a flat was available in those enviable times for less than the amount outstanding on most people's credit cards these days.

Once everyday household expenses had been budgeted for, readers were asked to consider their incidental expenses and holidays. It was all solid advice – though this, on clothes, may sound a jarring note today:

> Once the amount for clothes has been mutually agreed, it is better for the husband to hand the wife her portion in the form of a weekly or monthly allowance, to cover her own and, if necessary, the children's clothes. This is a more satisfactory arrangement than for the wife to have to ask her husband for the money whenever she requires to buy some new items of clothing.

Advice on buying furniture was similarly brisk and prescriptive, as if the author knew best:

- Go for good wood and good design; furniture is intended to serve as well as please.

- Seek strongly constructed pieces which stand firmly.

- Look not only at the overall finish, but also for a perfect fit at the joints.

- Try doors and drawers to check smooth operation and well-attached, easily gripped handles.

Terence Conran's shop, Habitat, which had opened its first outlet in London's Fulham Road in the same year (1964), would have instantly fitted the bill. However, there was something in the Teach Yourself tone that suggested such bold innovations would have to pass the test of time before the authors could wholeheartedly recommend them.

The prescriptive nature of *Teach Yourself Budgeting and Home Management* arguably reached extremes when it suggested not just that the "housewife has some degree of method in her daily routine" but that, with near military precision, she draw up a daily schedule. The book helpfully provides a sample:

7 am Make early morning tea.

7.15 Dress and get breakfast while husband does fire in sitting room.

7.45 Have breakfast.

8.00 Wash breakfast dishes (or put to soak); make beds and tidy bedroom; wipe out bath and basin.

8.30 Leave for work.

6pm Arrive home.

6.15 Prepare evening meal.

7.00 Serve meal.

7.30 Clear and wash up dishes. Lay breakfast, and make other preparations for morning.

This did not, incidentally include the two evenings a week spent on "general" house cleaning, ironing, mending etc., which were "fitted in when possible", and the weekend chores – laundry, shopping, "special" house cleaning, and extra cooking "planned to simplify mid-week meals".

You need a lie down after just reading it.

Nevertheless, the book was on hand to offer advice about how you could cut corners. One chapter dealt with the ergonomics of shopping and countered the received wisdom that held that women should go shopping every day:

> Many women have never quite thrown off the wartime habit of shopping personally for all their household goods and often weigh themselves down with heavy loads that add to fatigue and the physical strain of running a home.

Finally, when all the work was done there was time to relax and think about holidays. One of the burgeoning "holiday camps" was an option but ...

> It cannot really be said that the large commercially run holiday camps provide a cheap holiday, for the more ambitious ones cost 14 guineas a week, or even more, so for a family of four people an outlay of over £50 is needed for a week's holiday. There is the advantage, however, that the charge covers all entertainments.

And when you got back from holidays, what better way to acclimatise to the daily grind than by checking up on your domestic heating? *Teach*

Yourself Home Heating (1965) was waiting for you before you'd had time to unpack your bags – complete with historical prologue and lukewarm jokes:

> The Romans began the idea of heating our homes, for nothing could be draughtier than a toga.

The author, Alan White, made apt comparisons, however, between our approach to home heating and that of other countries, notably Canada, America and Scandinavia. To a British population that had endured the winter of 1963, the coldest on record since 1740, the point was well made:

> It is a painful voyage back to cold reality for the young export executive to return from the air-conditioned and centrally-heated luxury of even the smallest hotels of these countries, to be greeted by two lumps of fuel smouldering ineffectively on an open grate that has not changed appreciably since iron founding began. One could forgive his woollens clad wife if the warmth of her reception were somewhat chilled by weeks of manhandling coal lumps from an almost inaccessible storehouse, often in driving rain.

White moved effortlessly from the prosaic to the purple. A bald statistic that by the end of 1964 two million central heating systems had been installed in British homes rubbed shoulders with this:

Britain has been heated by radiant devices since the cave dweller learned to rub sticks together. This has inevitably led to the British style of architecture and decoration, in which each room has a centre piece, the fireplace, a focal point. Man has burnt cakes at it, toasted marshmallows or the seat of his trousers, young lovers have gazed into its flickering flames to vow eternal love, kettles have sung on the hobs of it and the gallimaufry of human existence has had it for an intimate and close spectator.

The cost of central heating was, of course, crucial. Mentioning no details whatsoever, White quoted a general figure of £450 as the cost of installation. Given that a small flat might cost £1,000 (*Teach Yourself Budgeting and Home Management*), this was a hefty whack. He justifies it as follows:

Many a young man has crossed a young lady off his list when he discovers that her dainty appetite is for the high priced food, caviar, pheasant, champagne – (a bottle contains as many calories as a stove burning for ten minutes, and is much more stimulating ...) Yet the same young man will heat his flat in St James's by small amounts of the most expensive fuel.

Cave dweller in northern Europe. Executive in St James's. The Teach Yourself books were nothing if not inclusive.

As living standards rose, new titles appeared with the aim of satisfying them. *Teach Yourself Complete Meals* (1966), for example, took cookery to a new level. It assumed that the reader (a woman, naturally) was familiar with the rudiments of cookery – perhaps she had even read the pre-war trailblazer, *Teach Yourself to Cook* (1938) – but that she now wanted to plan and prepare more imaginative dishes. For her, the mere taste of food would be enhanced by texture, colour, presentation and contrasts:

> A soft bland dish of meat in gravy would be more appetising after a tangy shrimp-stuffed tomato than after a creamy soup.

With rationing and food shortages things of the past, she could now raise her game. Mere staples could be balanced by life's luxuries – by exotic spices and herbs, by garlic bread and ratatouille, by moussaka and spaghetti Margherita. New words were entering her culinary vocabulary – for many, new produce, too. There was talk of avocado with vinaigrette, of ragout and pissaladiere. When the granddaddy of celebrity chefs, Keith Floyd, was a youngster plotting a British culinary revolution, he could well have gained confidence from reading a book like this with its talk of piperade and cassoulet. The early appearance of dishes he was to popularise twenty years later on TV would have proved to him he was on to something big.

When the author proposed a series of alternative Christmas menus to replace the traditional turkey and bread sauce, her roast goose with orange sauce, cream of pea soup, orange savoury rice, zabaglione and chocolate pots could have come from the pages of a Nigel Slater cookery book today. No colour photographs and gastroporn then, however, just solid accessible menus. In its way, the book was a minor culinary revolution of its time.

R & R

The Teach Yourself series continued to add titles to its growing sports and recreation section, each one brimming with the characteristic dose of enthusiasm. *Teach Yourself Archery* (1961) was typical:

> Drawing a bow at a venture? Yes, that is what you will be doing when you take up the sport of archery, but without the element of risk. Archery is an exciting, fascinating adventure and once you have fallen under its spell, you will never want to give it up. Archery is a health-giving sport. It takes you out of doors into the fields and is a complete relaxation from work. Worries are banished from the mind.

Archery, we were told has a long history beginning with, erm, early man at the dawn of time:

> The prehistoric drawings on the walls of caves of men with bows and arrows are said to be 20,000 years old.

No sport for sissies

Archery is no longer a game for young ladies to be played on the vicarage lawn but has become once again a virile, manly sport.

Teach Yourself Archery, 1961

Queen Elizabeth I was said to have been a good shot, and the sport was very popular with young ladies during the reign of Queen Victoria. Yet the "virile" nature of the sport needed to be stressed. A brief paragraph on the bow and arrow's suitability for jungle warfare ("they can kill silently and swiftly at close quarters") underlined the manly element and, perhaps, its increasing popularity:

> As a sport archery is growing with astonishing rapidity for this Atomic Age.

The series catered for the everyday sports as well, whether in *Teach Yourself Squash Rackets* (1968) or *Teach Yourself Table Tennis* (1966), where it was gratifying for once not to read that "prehistoric cave paintings suggest that primitive man may have played a form of ping pong".

> ### The etiquette of winter sports
>
> *Ladies should be guided by the sort of evening wear expected of their menfolk. Where a dark suit is mandatory après-ski slacks, however glamorous, are unlikely to be looked upon with favour in the dining-room, although such outfits are very much de rigueur for an after-dinner entertainment in even the smartest of hotels and night-spots.*
>
> *Teach Yourself Skiing*, 1967

An interesting title appeared in 1963, pointing the way towards the gym culture of today. It is well known that the diet of the 1950s was thought to have been the healthiest of modern times. Food rationing, particularly of butters and fats, and the virtual absence of ready meals and highly processed food ensured the nation's diet was far from self-indulgent. Pictures of ordinary men stripped to the waist on holiday, for example, or workmen repairing the roads show uniformly lean physiques and trim figures. Obesity was not the national epidemic it has become today.

Had the Teach Yourself editors foreseen a time, however, when increased standards of living might take their toll on the country's health and fitness? *Teach Yourself Physical Fitness* (1963) hinted at it:

Not long ago the safety of a nation and the freedom of its people in an internationally dangerous world depended largely on the ability of at least its young men to bear arms in case of need ... It is no longer obvious that a nation of physically fit citizens, able to take the field, is more likely to survive in a future war than one defended by a handful of experts and one more reason for cultivating such fitness is gone or going.

In many other smaller ways the book was ahead of its time. Walking and jogging, for example, "on unfrequented undulating roads or, best of all, on downland turf" were recommended as exercises that everyone could take up without the bother of buying specialist gear. The book also encouraged parents to bring up their children with an enjoyment of exercise, letting them take occasional risks in life rather than mollycoddling them and allowing them to retreat to the TV.

The emergence of the couch potato generation

Not long ago hoops, tops, skipping ropes, rubber balls, boxes on wheels, "diabolo" cones, roller skates, and other simple apparatus turned London back streets into open air gymnasia and at school inspections the physique of children who "lived rough" and played in such streets

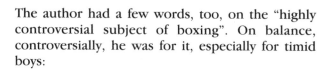

> *compared very favourably with that of*
> *others more comfortably and "respectably"*
> *brought up. Today the motor vehicle tends*
> *to monopolise the streets and the "telly"*
> *keeps many children passively watching*
> *indoors in the none-too-long hours*
> *between school and bed.*
>
> *Teach Yourself Physical Fitness*, 1963

The author had a few words, too, on the "highly controversial subject of boxing". On balance, controversially, he was for it, especially for timid boys:

> When he learns to put himself into a posture of determined defence and to divert a blow with his right hand he begins to feel he is not a worm. Perhaps he may feel he has some guts after all. This means that his starved self-respect will get a little badly needed nourishment.

He also believed that skill in boxing will "stand him in good stead in years to come". How? Well, he added, with a hint of understatement, "violence is not unknown in our streets".

The middle aged were advised to exercise to avoid flabbiness and ill health, and the author had the usual words of wisdom for the housewife:

If a wife does her own housework and does not employ too many labour-saving devices for the sweeping and polishing jobs – as opposed to those of the sink and the standing in queues – some excellent exercise for limbs and trunk will come her way.

Unfortunately, we have no idea how this useful and very helpful advice went down with the housewife of the time.

If the Teach Yourself series encouraged people to take strenuous exercise, it also taught them how to relax in their spare time with civilised leisure pursuits. *Teach Yourself Drawing and Painting* (1966) brought the two earlier volumes of *Teach Yourself Perspective Drawing* (1953) and *Teach Yourself Painting For Pleasure* (1953) together, bringing readers right up to date with the Pop Art revolution but leaving them in no doubt as to what the author really thought about the artists:

The Pop-artists claim that a commercial pack, a slot-machine or a drainpipe are as fitting subjects for a work of art as any of those which conform to orthodox standards. This is true. But it is also true that only in the hands of the sincere artist can these elements be lifted from their commonplace existence into works which can justly claim aesthetic value.

YOUR EYES ARE GETTING HEAVY

Relaxation was certainly to be had from studying, in your own time, books like *History of Music* (1961), *Guidebook to the Drama* (1960), *Indoor Plants* (1968) and *Birds; A Primer of Ornithology* (1962), but a different type of relaxation was promoted in 1966 by F. N. Sutherland. In *Teach Yourself to Relax*, he proposed something altogether different from winding down after a hard day. Just as *Physical Fitness* had heralded the age of the gym, the workout, and even the personal trainer, this book inaugurated, in its own popular way, the "mind, body, spirit" age of holistic therapies and homeopathic alternatives to tension and depression. Its approach was more akin to yoga (not as commonplace then as now) and thus came with reassurances to the sceptical:

> Relaxation is not just a fad of some crank, but rather a technique which has proved itself.

Or:

> Relaxation therapy is not an airy-fairy theory with no scientific foundation, created by some theorist who was unwilling to face realities. It is a scientifically proved method of treatment.

And Sutherland makes grand claims for it:

> If you practise the technique outlined in this book you will find a way to face life without

strain, tension, and worry. You will find release
from nervous and muscular tension. You will
discover a new zest for living because you will
have been directed towards a new true peace
of mind.

The aim of the book was to get beyond drugs-
based "cures" for stress and mental disorder, and
promote health through natural remedies:

It has been estimated that there are three
million people with handicapping neurosis in
Great Britain alone. The prevalence of
emotional illness can be seen by the extent to
which drugs are being used in this country.
Last year [1965] 15,800,000 barbiturate pills
at a cost of £1,700,000 were prescribed under
the National Health Service.

This new approach was, in short, a way of
promoting physical *and* mental well-being and an
inner harmony that bordered on the spiritual – a
quantum shift from the "physical jerks", the
"downland walking", and the ergonomic
household chores of the *Physical Fitness* volume.
Perhaps it was with *Teach Yourself to Relax* that
the series first taught itself how to be in tune with
the Age of Aquarius. Certainly without it there
could have been no *Teach Yourself Tantric Sex*
(2002) and no *Teach Yourself Ayurveda* (2007).

But, and it was a fairly big but, the book was
not a syncretistic mix of yogic and tantric
philosophies, and it did not draw on the wisdom of

ancient Eastern religions. The book was unashamedly Christian in its worldview. Sutherland makes that much clear:

> Long ago I had accepted the Christian faith myself, and as a result had come to see that the only way to a real, fully integrated personality was when one accepted the Christian faith and truth.

This was in the grand old tradition of the series founder, Leonard Cutts, himself a deeply pious man who saw the Christian faith as central to life itself, and the subjects he promoted as partial reflections of the abundant life Christianity offered. Sutherland's envoi says it all:

> May you indeed discover the true peace of mind that comes to those who are able to relax, and find a new peace of mind in your experience of God.

In the light of that, one suspects that twenty-first-century commissioning editors would have had a challenge on their hands persuading Leonard Cutts to greenlight *Teach Yourself Tantric Sex* – and possibly *Ayurveda*, *Flirting*, and *How to Win at Horse Racing* – but they would undoubtedly have seen eye to eye with him in concluding that every text not only had to be authoritative but in tune with its time. Besides, Leonard Cutts had always been the first to accept that, as times change, books themselves must, however slowly, change with them.

CHAPTER V

THE SAMOANS HAVE A WORD FOR IT

SPONGEBAG IN HAND

Cenedl heb iaith, cenedl heb galon

How true. And very much a principle that has guided the Teach Yourself language series throughout its seventy years, making it the leading foreign language teaching publisher in Britain today.

Should you be unfamiliar with the Welsh tag in the original, the above means "A nation without language, a nation without heart". Both John T. Bowen and T. J. Rhys Jones, joint authors of *Teach Yourself Welsh* (1960), planned their book for two quite specific audiences:

> When you have worked conscientiously through this book, you should be able to speak

Welsh, understand Welsh conversation and read an ordinary Welsh book. Is that sufficient reward? Surely yes, but more will be added. If you are a Welshman, then you will be a proper Welshman, standing on his own feet, with his own language, his own heritage and not just a strange kind of Englishman.

In other words, whether you were the prodigal son of Owen Glendower, the dispossessed daughter of ancient Cymru, or simply a general reader hoping to puff on a "sigaret", sip a "coffi" and spend a quiet half-hour reading a "nofel" while stroking your goatee alongside academic and media types on Aberystwyth's Corniche, this was the book for you.

However, Welsh or not, you had to be prepared for hard work. Nothing (especially not the mastery of a foreign tongue) was to be achieved without effort and dedication. The over-arching *Teach Yourself to Learn a Language* (1965) by P.J.T. Glendening spelled that out clearly enough:

Alas! Man has for ever been seeking the impossible, since well before the medieval alchemists, and more time and energy have gone into seeking short-cuts than would have taken seekers all the long way round, had they attempted to go this way in the first instance.

As a consequence, the author advised that all books bearing more than a passing similarity to the following titles should be avoided at all costs:

"Welsh in a Week", "French in Five Days without a Master", "German without Grammar", and "Fluent Finnish in a Fortnight". The necessary requirements for fluency in any language were – along with "intelligent hard work" – boundless enthusiasm and what was called "the correct psychological outlook". With those boxes duly ticked, the beginner could ... well ... begin.

Yet even beginning meant coming to grips with mood, declension, nominal concord, past participle, subjunctive, predicate and similar grammatical terms, which the author cheerfully informed us were "only the bare essentials". And the complexity did not stop there. At a time when discs or tapes were not included with the books, the section on pronunciation had to be dealt with in written text and in diagrams. Without a basic grounding in phonetics and at least a familiarity with the anatomy of the mouth, terms such as "labial", "bi-labial", "palato-alveolar", "glottal", "fricative" and "plosive" were meaningless. To be frank, it is hard to imagine who must have bought the book (or rather who must have read it after purchase), apart from those competent in linguistics in the first place.

True, the book sets out to explain the ideas behind the terms, but realistically it would have required such sustained and applied effort that only the hyper-diligent would have persisted. Most would have found the concepts so far removed from what they had understood by "learning French" that, one suspects, they would have thrown in the towel very early on.

However, a discussion on the criteria for judging what constituted a "major" and a "minor" language threw up some interesting ideas, some of which were very much products of their time:

> Shall our criterion perhaps be the ability of the language concerned to cope with ideas? Have you heard the argument that there is no fear of the H-bomb being produced independently by many countries, as few modern languages are able to cope with the complexities involved? (this argument has even been used in connection with Russia, which brands it as wishful thinking).

Teach Yourself to Learn a Language was unashamedly a book about theory. If you wanted practical expertise you had to consult the mainstream language volumes that, from the outset, were an important and highly popular component of the Teach Yourself series.

The list in 1940 was small and included only *Teach Yourself French*, *Teach Yourself Everyday French*, *Teach Yourself German* and *Teach Yourself Spanish*. The content was inescapably traditional but authors tried to package it in an informal and non-threatening way. *Teach Yourself Everyday French* (1940), for example, begins as follows (this did, incidentally, pass for informal in those days):

> At the age of eleven I remember complaining bitterly of the intricacies of French grammar.

The schoolmaster, whose heavy duty it was to instruct me in the rudiments of the Gallic tongue, pulled my ear firmly and retorted that, on the contrary, the main rules of the language could be set down on a single sheet of notepaper. He was a keen fisherman in his spare time, and consequently prone to exaggeration. Nevertheless ... French grammar is comparatively simple.

The point of this book was to build on the foundations laid in *Teach Yourself French* (1938) and to enable the student "to blossom out". Part of this involved mastering the difference between "business and private correspondence" and writing appropriately:

Your maiden aunt may well write: "I was delighted to get your letter and learn of all your doings" (ie. those you judged it prudent to tell her). The Inland Revenue Officer, on the other hand, is likely to send you a more alarming missive beginning brusquely: "Yours to hand of the 28th ult., etc.".

Standards of general literacy, it was clear, were assumed to be high:

Anybody can read Galsworthy or Kipling without preliminary explanation. To make a start with Chaucer is a very different matter. In like manner André Maurois is far easier to tackle than Rabelais or François Villon.

All very well, but the conversational banter that passed for everyday French in this book was about as strange as anything to appear in François Rabelais and François Villon put together. Here we are invited into Anne and Victor's hotel room on the morning after their arrival in Paris. To spare indelicate questions, they are a *married* couple.

LESSON X

Translation Exercise 10 (a)

(It is eight o'clock in the morning. A bedside table separates the twin beds. Anne, stifling a yawn, sits up in bed. All night she has worn a hair-net, the better to preserve the set of her "wave". Victor is still asleep. She looks at him, or rather at a lock of hair, the only part of his head which the bedclothes do not hide.)

A. Victor! Wake up!

V. He?

A. Come on. Wake up. It's gone eight o'clock. There's no need to ask if you slept well!

(Victor stretches to unstiffen his limbs. Then he runs his hand through his hair. Seeing that he is on the point of dozing off again she throws a pillow at his head.)

V. *(leaping from his bed)* I'll pay you for that! *(he begins to tickle her)*

A. *(convulsed with laughter)* Ow! No! Mercy! You're hurting me. Stop! I can't bear any more! You'll tear my pyjamas. I only bought them yesterday and they cost me a fortune. They're the very latest thing.

V. Cost you? You know very well that I shall pay for them.

A. (*getting up and putting on a wrap*) Draw back the curtains, dear.

V. (*by the window*) What a grand morning! I feel ten years younger to-day.

A. You look well, there's no denying.

V. I feel as fit as a fiddle. For once, at least, I shall take pleasure in doing my physical jerks.

A. Before you begin, will you turn on my bath?

V. (*having turned on the taps*) My word! It runs fast. It's like a river in spate! By the way, when we go out this morning, will you remind me that I must buy a cake of soap? I was in such a hurry before our departure that I forgot they don't give you any in foreign hotels.

(*A. goes to have her bath. V. does some loosening up exercises. Then he stands near the window breathing to the full extent of his lungs. That done he goes towards the bathroom.*)

V. (*knocking on the door*) Hurry up, Anne. I want to shave.

A. Another two minutes.

(Having walked up and down with ever-growing impatience, Victor unhooks the telephone receiver.)

V. This is No. 76. Will you bring coffee and rolls for two please? (*in a lower tone*) In a quarter of an hour.

(This little scheme is successful. Anne rushes into the room and begins to dress. Victor goes into the bathroom, spongebag in hand. Just as the chambermaid arrives, carrying the breakfast on a tray, Victor, in his shirt-sleeves, is on the point of putting on his coat, whilst his wife is putting the finishing touches to her make-up.)

The format of the lessons and exercises was simple but demanding. First the reader would study a basic vocabulary list (including such essential phrases as "to berth aft of the funnel", "to smuggle in goods" and "to buy on a rising market"), then he or she was asked to translate this one-sided telephone conversation into French:

That's just our luck! For six months we have been working like blazes, and the publisher to whom we submitted our manuscript informs us very politely that a work which treats exactly of the same subject as ours is going to appear next week. He advises me not to allow myself to be discouraged and tells me that I shall do well. To hear him speak, one would think everything is going swimmingly. I have half a mind to go

on strike. Don't get worked up? You mean well,
my friend, but if you talk to me in that fashion
I shall beg you to be good enough to hop it!

This sounds positively colloquial when compared
to Exercise 18 later in the book when the reader is
expected to translate this snatch of "everyday"
dialogue into French:

"Here is the meteorological information over
the Landes, captain. Practical ceiling of 700
metres. Sky cloudy."

"Right, we're going."

The take-off is effected (reflexive) at ten
o'clock. The aeronautical light-houses of
several airports are picked up in turn. Then
the clouds come closer (se reserrer). Bordeaux
is descried through the clouds, but soon after
wireless connection becomes difficult.

Teach Yourself Spanish (1939) was written by the
same author as *Teach Yourself Everyday French*,
N. Scarlyn Wilson, who admitted he was copying
the methods he had previously used but defended
himself against the charge of plagiarism on the
grounds that, "as the lunatic very luminously
observed: 'If I can't bang my head against my own
mantlepiece, whose mantlepiece can I bang it
against?'" And although the book aimed at ...

steering a middle course between dreary
sentences about Grandmother's thimble and
phrases of idiomatic slang ...

... some of the translation exercises did not always live up to the promise:

- I bought this tobacco pouch two years ago.
- I am very fond of music; have the goodness to turn on the wireless.
- I should very much like to wear socks with zip-fasteners.
- It is useless to tell me you have nothing to declare.

Where socks with zip-fasteners might be bought outside the red light area of Amsterdam was not explained.

Sadly *Teach Yourself Dutch* (1941) was unable to offer enlightenment. It aimed at "those who wish to acquire a knowledge of Dutch by private study" and made it clear from the start that extra effort would be needed to master the language. The child at school, and to some extent the adult at evening class, had the luxury of being guided and helped to understand by a teacher. The solitary reader did not have this advantage so had to look elsewhere for help. In all the language books, readers were encouraged to back up their own private efforts by reading newspapers and listening to radio broadcasts (Messrs Bowen and Rhys Jones recommended singing along to Welsh hymns on TV, for instance). Essentially, however, students were on their own and, as a result, proficiency relied on no-frills, grammatically-based hard graft. You were, as it said on the cover, teaching yourself. If you stayed the course (with its conjugations, declensions, agreements and irregular verbs) you learned the language, or as *Teach Yourself Russian* (1943) put it:

> A student of average intelligence, who is willing to attend and persevere, can soon acquire a working knowledge of the language. If, after making this start, you continue to study and manage occasionally to meet Russian people, or can spend a holiday in the Soviet Union, you will eventually get a really useful knowledge of Russian, which in the post-war world may well prove of great cultural and commercial importance and become as popular as the languages more generally studied now.

Press on, then, with translating "the captain's dog", "the watchman's stick", "the steamer's rudder", and "the grandson's apple", and you would soon be reading Nikolai Gogol and Ivan Turgenev.

A practically identical form of words prefaced *Teach Yourself Italian* (1943), stressing that, while this was in no way a formal grammar book, it nonetheless contained the grammatical points essential to mastery of the spoken and written word. The rest was up to close study, memory and regular practice:

> You cannot teach yourself a language by fits and starts; you must make up your mind to go slowly and steadily, always being sure of one lesson before passing on to the next, and you

will soon surprise yourself with the progress you are making.

In retrospect, books like this were brave undertakings. Making "progress" in German and Italian in the early 1940s would have been mirrored by the "progress" the Axis powers were making towards El Alamein and, for many, learning the languages of Rommel and Il Duce would have held only marginal attractions. The decision to publish such books, therefore, was a bold down payment on the notion of a shared cultural future in more pacific times than the 1940s.

ATTEND AND PERSEVERE

Understanding and speaking the words were sometimes only part of the whole process of learning the language. Particularly with the Middle Eastern and Asian languages, a familiarity with the national and regional culture was a prerequisite of complete (or even partial) mastery. Take this, from *Teach Yourself Arabic* (1943):

> The Arab sits on the floor and eats with his fingers; when he wants to eat or sleep his food is brought to him. The result is that many words, indispensable in English, scarcely occur in accounts of native life. For "table" Syria uses an Italian, Egypt a Greek, and Mesopotamia a Persian word. This book is an introduction to written Arabic which is understood from the Atlantic to the frontiers of

Persia. It will not help a man to talk to a crossing-sweeper the day of his arrival but it will quicken his progress in talking after the first month or so.

This cultural element possibly explained the choice of Arabic phrases for translation – gnomic utterances to a Westerner today but doubtless understood instinctively by a native-speaker then:

- Relatives are scorpions.
- The learned are heirs of the prophets.
- The vices of the elect are the virtues of the mob.
- The honour of a man is his sons.
- The seamstresses went away from our town and returned to their native land.

Teach Yourself More German (1946) made equally precise social and cultural assumptions of its readers, as this exercise in translation shows:

Mr Miller goes every day to the office. He catches the 9 o'clock train to Waterloo, shows his season-ticket at the barrier and goes down the moving stairs to travel by tube to the City. He finds the office clean and tidy, as it has been swept and dusted by the charwoman.

That was just the start of it. Before long we were dealing with the conversational niceties surrounding a game of golf and were expected to translate the subtleties of the following dialogue between Dr Tellerbach, a seasoned golfer, and Ann, a beginner. The scene; a fairway in Scotland ("the home of golf"):

> ANN. I cannot hope to compete with you. You are much too good for me. A game like this cannot be very exciting for you.
>
> Dr T. Why ever not? In golf a weaker player doesn't hinder a better one in the least, and even if he does, the charm of this unique game does not reside in the competition of physical prowess, but in walking in the open air and in spiritual contact with kindred spirits – especially when the spirit is a charming young lady.
>
> ANN. Heavens above! If you talk like that, my dear Doctor, I shall find it utterly impossible to keep my eye on the ball, as my attention will be hovering between it and my spiritual effect on you.
>
> Dr T. (*with a laugh*) You need not worry about that. Wooden peg, sand or rubber tee?

Suspecting that the good doctor probably said that to all the girls, we were, sadly, denied any ensuing conversation. By way of compensation, however, we were presented (for translation purposes) with this exciting snatch of conversation between Andrew, Jean and Peter Hamilton, involving Peter's purchase of a state-of-the-art "wireless-set":

P.H. Do you know what? I have a surprise for you!

A.H. All right, fire away, we are all ears.

P.H. I've bought a wireless-set.

J.H. Heavens above! What for?

P.H. To listen-in with. Didn't you say last night that you missed the news from London?

A.H. What sort of set is it – a crystal-set, a portable or –

P.H. Nothing of the sort! It is a 5-valve set with indoor aerial and all the latest devices.

J.H. Do you have a battery or those awful accumulators that have to be charged every now and then?

P.H. Good Lord no! It's an all-mains receiving set. You plug in, tune in, turn the jolly old knobs and there you are!

Simple. The wireless as linguistic metaphor. All you needed to do was follow the Teach Yourself steps and, given time and practice, you would be a competent foreign language speaker. Just turn the jolly old knobs, in a manner of speaking, and there you were. What exactly Dr Tellerbach was doing on the fairways of St Andrews, by the way, and indeed what Peter Hamilton and his friends were doing buying state-of-the-art wirelesses in post-war Germany while all eyes were on the Nuremberg Trials was not explained.

There were other mysteries confronting the would-be linguist. Take the paradox of Malay, for instance:

> Malay is an easy language. Bafflingly easy. At the end of ten weeks you feel that you know all that there is to be known. At the end of ten years, you know that you never will.

The author of *Teach Yourself Malay* (1947), M. B. Lewis, had the right idea – the Teach Yourself idea – for going about things:

> People will tell you that it is possible to "pick up" Malay in a couple of months. So it is, if you are going to be content with the 'bazaar' Malay of the sea-ports. The ideal method of learning Malay – or any other living language – is to combine book work with practical work. You will understand much more of what you hear around you if you know, from book work, what to listen for.

Before beginners could aspire to the Olympian heights of fluency they had to go by the foothills of everyday translation. "I must buy a hat for Torsten" or "Parcels go via Tilbury" were pretty rudimentary, it has to be said. Yet they were a start.

The *Teach Yourself Russian Phrasebook* (1949) built on its earlier counterpart *Teach Yourself Russian*. The compilers, however, writing six years before the Soviet Union became a joint signatory to the Warsaw Pact, could hardly have foreseen the realities of the upcoming Cold War, and so contented themselves with broad generalisations:

> Go to Russia as to any other country, dear Traveller, acting as an ambassador of friendship to a friendly, kindly people. Wear your heart on your sleeve and a smile on your lips; put good humour into your talk and simple courtesy into your behaviour: you will be amply rewarded by the warm welcome you will receive, and your visit to the U.S.S.R. will become a rich memory stored for your future enjoyment.

The following year, J. R. Firth of the School of Oriental and African Studies in London began his preface to *Teach Yourself Hindustani* (1950) with the following:

> This book is based on material left by the late Dr Grahame Bailey, the well-known Indianist, who died in 1942. Among his posthumous papers there were at least two versions of what he intended should become a grammar and language course of Hindustani.

He went on:

> The Romanic orthography employed is the outcome of my own work on an All-India alphabet ... I am responsible for the introduction to the spelling and pronunciation, which should promote ease

and speed of learning, make for early fluency, and pave the way for the transition to the Indian systems of writing, both Persi-Arabic and Devanagari.

Whichever way you looked at it, the book contained the fruit of a lifetime's loving and devoted study by linguists of the highest calibre. A bargain at seven shillings and sixpence. And, by the way, in the same book you could also inform your Indian host that "the curry's got burnt and stuck to the pan" or, in cases of real need, that "London's nine times as big as Birmingham".

Similarly useful phrases were on offer in the *Teach Yourself Spanish Phrasebook* (1954, revised 1965). Covering travel, food, money, health and recreations, it had all the traveller needed to get by on holiday. It made no claims to be either a grammar or a language teaching aid, simply a guide to put in your pocket or rucksack and to help you out in an emergency should you "have forgotten what you once learnt at school or on active service".

Essential phrases

- *This hat with black feathers does not match my brown coat.*
- *I am going to clap my hands to see whether the night watchman comes along.*
- *I was a private in an armoured formation.*

Teach Yourself Spanish Phrasebook, 1954

Its Italian counterpart, the *Teach Yourself Italian Phrasebook* (1954), was just as helpful in everyday situations and, it being 1954 when Italian food was not so readily available in Britain, had useful information for the first-time traveller:

> In Milan there is a special savoury rice, coloured golden yellow with saffron, in Naples a delicious dish called "*pizza*", in Rome another called "*mozzarella*", which must be tasted to be believed.

Useful advice for the first-time spaghetti eater

Just insert the fork into the middle of the mass and roll a prudent number of strands round the fork with a rapid movement, then thrust the little bundle quickly into the mouth, without caring if a few lengths hang out. These may be quietly sucked in – and in any case everyone else is doing the same. A little gay insouciance is all that is needed; concentration and anxiety are entirely out of place.

Teach Yourself Italian Phrasebook, 1954

The phrasebook promised an anxiety-free experience from the moment the traveller arrived:

Once he steps out of the train into Italy, holding his book in his hand and his smile on his face, the rest will come easily.

Less easy perhaps was the mastery of "the eternal mother tongue of all true religion" – though *Teach Yourself Hebrew* (1955) attempted it. Since it was directed primarily at the student of biblical Hebrew, it was hardly surprising that, instead of traditional words like "newspaper", "train", "bottle" and so on, this specialist volume listed "sin", "burnt offering", "seraph", "Pharaoh", "firmament", and "handmaid" as everyday items of vocabulary.

FURTHER AFIELD

The addition of *Teach Yourself Afrikaans* (1957) and *Teach Yourself Danish* (1958) brought the total list of language books to thirty-four by 1958. There would be scope for many more – for the *Teach Yourself Serbo-Croatian Phrase Book* (1961), for example:

For surprise and variety Yugoslavia – the land of the South Slavs – can have no European rival.

A brief survey of Yugoslavia's history takes the country to the end of the Austro-Hungarian Empire and to 1918. The introduction passes over the country's social and political evolution since, mentioning only that:

The successive incursions of rapacious neighbours not only formed the astounding resilience of the Yugoslav character but left their mark in a rich variety of linguistic, architectural, sartorial, and culinary forms.

The author, Viola Ellis, glancingly mentions the darker side of Balkan nationalism but, by nature irrepressibly optimistic, she prefers to accentuate the positive and comes down unequivocally on the side of warm welcomes and native hospitality:

All these differences, though often exploited in the past to provoke fratricidal bitterness, have fused now into an enthusiastic, recognizable unity that is heart-warming to encounter. Everywhere the visitor finds true Balkan hospitality. Only stiffness on his part can prevent the spontaneous warmth of a genuine welcome. On the other hand, an acquaintance with their language, however tentative, always evokes delighted encouragement.

The phrases touch on the usual practicalities of travel, accommodation, shopping and eating but devote an unusually large number of pages to sports. In the gymnastics and athletics section, for example, there is a full list of all the gymnastic equipment to be found in any serious gymnasium, while the riding, hunting and shooting section has a selection of essential phrases for the tourist wanting to make a mark:

- Where can I buy a rifle?

- Would you care to come with me to shoot hares?

- Where is my whip?

- Please harness the white horse for me.

- Did you get a good bag?

The section on boxing helpfully deals with the technicalities of bantam-weight, feather-weight and heavy-weight, and assumes some level of participation in the sport with phrases like "Did your friend defend his title?" It assumes the reader is an active individual, ready to get his ice-skates on one day and take to the ski-slopes the next, rounding off the week's activities with a spot of mountaineering:

- Do I need a rope and an axe?

- We might lose our way in the blizzard.

- Let's watch the sunrise from the peak.

And, by way of relaxation after all the hard work:

- Can we get some refreshments at the alpine dairy?

If mountaineering and the weather should dry up as conversation pieces, words and phrases were on hand for the militarily inclined. Although phrases like "Did you ever take part in an air raid?" could reasonably be assumed to be conversation stoppers in most everyday circumstances, the

Serbo-Croation Phrase Book actively encouraged them, suggesting other useful springboards for small talk such as:

- I was a parachutist.
- The enemy is retreating.
- Were you a submarine captain?

Here's one that might guarantee keen interest from any off-duty secret policeman on Cold War alert:

- How many men-of-war are lying in the harbour?

Teach Yourself Icelandic (1961) took us back to less controversial ground and, among other things, to the literary heritage of the Norse Sagas and to the influence of Norse on the shaping of many everyday English words. Interestingly, and practically alone among Teach Yourself language books, it recommended children's books as an excellent way of building up skills in a language.

Teach Yourself was largely aimed at the general reader but occasionally had the specialist in mind. How else to explain the appearance in 1962 of *Teach Yourself Samoan*? With much of the islands' history, traditions and folklore passed down the generations by word of mouth, written Samoan clearly posed an enormous challenge to a general readership. Only those with a particular interest in the region and its culture would, in the normal run of things, have had any reason to be drawn to the

Samoan language. For such persons, however, this was the book.

> It is believed that a careful study of the Lessons will equip him with all the knowledge required to read as much written Samoan as is likely to swim into his ken and, with practice, to carry on conversation with Samoans on all subjects he is likely to find it necessary to discuss.

Western Samoa's achievement of independence from New Zealand in the same year as the book's publication was certainly well timed but, even with this coincidence of events, the book was almost certainly destined for the specialist market alone.

Maltese, like Samoan, statistically a minority language, also got the full Teach Yourself treatment. Joseph Aquilina, author of *Teach Yourself Maltese* (1965), sold the interest factor for all it was worth – which was considerable. Inhabited by the pre-Phoenicians ("whose megalithic temples of 2400 BC dot the island"), Malta became a Phoenician colony around 800 BC and a Carthaginian colony a century later. Then came:

> ... the Romans (218 BC), the Arabs (870– 1090), the Normans, Suabians, Angevins, Aragonese and Castilians (1090–1530), the Order of St John (1530–1798), the French (1798–1800) and last the British (1800–1964).

And all that by the first page. The linguistic point
being that:

> ... spoken Maltese, like modern English, which
> is basically Anglo-Saxon where Maltese is
> largely Semitic, has so many loan-words. But
> so strong is the Semitic morphology of the
> language that these have been adapted to
> Maltese morphological word-patterns.

Which is quite a mouthful in any language – and
serves to underline not only that the Teach
Yourself books could be mini works of scholarship
in their own right, but also that they could cater for
readers with an already well-developed
understanding of linguistics.

Teach Yourself Bengali (1965) was a similarly
scholarly tome clearly intended for an experienced
student familiar with the past frequentative tense,
the future imperative tense, the second person
inferior, the third person honorific, and so on. It
was the product of a collaboration with the
Language School in Darjeeling, whose staff (many
of them Christian ministers) were pioneers in
modern linguistics. Perhaps it was this
combination of scholarship and Christian ethics
that appealed to the editor Leonard Cutts:

> ... whose breath-taking letter accepting the
> book before he had seen it, [wrote the author
> in the preface] could not fail to stimulate one
> who is very conscious of his limitations.

By the time *Teach Yourself Indonesian* appeared in 1965, the Teach Yourself language list had increased impressively, with Chinese, Czech, Esperanto, Hausa, Irish, Japanese, Latvian, modern Persian, Polish, Portuguese, Swahili, and Turkish joining forty-seven other titles in a series that had established itself as a first port of call for millions of readers seeking to acquire a foreign language.

The early books made it clear from the outset that they were not to be regarded as magic wands. Readers would get out of them only what they put in. With the right attitude, sufficient application, and a lot of practice (preferably in the company of native speakers but also, later, with the accompanying audio cassettes), readers would eventually succeed in mastering their chosen language. And mastering the language, the editors believed, meant getting close to the very heart of a culture and a people. As *Teach Yourself Colloquial Arabic; The Living Language of Egypt* (1962) had put it:

> No reasonable man, however, in whatever homogenous society, is anxious to talk like a book, and the language that the same educated Egyptian uses on return to the bosom of his family or generally with his compatriots is quite other than that in which he addresses non-Egyptians. The second language is wholly Egyptian and it is exclusively with it that this book is concerned.

PEOPLE ON THE MOVE

If the Teach Yourself editors had a soft spot for the specialist and the dedicated linguist, they also had an eye for the mass market which, thanks to peacetime prosperity and regeneration, was just around the corner. Among the growing possibilities available to all in the post-war years was the chance to travel abroad – without a rifle or a parachute – as a simple tourist. And as the late 1950s gave way to the 1960s, the availability of cheap foreign travel grew. The family that had been happy to spend a week at an English seaside resort in summer – in a purpose-built holiday camp, perhaps, and in driving rain and howling gales – was beginning to look at possibilities further afield. With the Russian cosmonaut Yuri Gagarin blasted into space in the first year of the new decade (blazing a trail pioneered months earlier by his fellow primate, "Ham" the chimp), there was now no stopping any of us from daring to venture anywhere we might choose. Indeed, when the following year the recently elected US President John F. Kennedy declared America's intention to put a man on the *moon* before the end of the decade, foreign destinations on mere Earth seemed decidedly tame by comparison.

All the while, tiny fishing villages like Torremolinos and Benidorm on the Spanish Costas were reshaping themselves to cater for the growing influx of tourists attracted by the prospect of cheap air travel, good weather, and pints of terrible beer at pre-war prices. The first Boeing 737, one of the most popular passenger jet aircrafts of all time, made its appearance in the spring of 1967 and the package holiday explosion was well and truly primed.

Of course, *Teach Yourself Spanish*, *Italian*, *French*, *Greek*, *Maltese*, and *Turkish* were all on hand to enable first-time visitors or seasoned returnees to those respective countries to order paella and souvlaki, spaghetti and bouillabaise – plus the ubiquitous steak and chips – at all points east of Gibraltar. It would be some years before Teach Yourself writers and translators would have to contend with the linguistic impossibility of the "all-day breakfast", since in the early days this had thankfully not yet reached the apogee of its culinary evolution. But that is another story entirely.

Throughout the 1960s, 1970s and 1980s, the Teach Yourself approach to language remained largely the same, offering the reader a general grounding in the grammatical structure of the language and then practice in a number of tried and tested situations in the hotel, at the station, at the cinema, at the market and so on. There were no more encounters with Aryan professors on the golf links of St Andrews, no more idle chats about small arms and military rank, and thankfully no return of the insufferably smug Anne and Victor. Instead, we had everyday conversations about the everyday practicalities of life. However, as the end of the century and the millennium drew closer, so the Teach Yourself packaging of its language courses dramatically altered. The phrase books and the grammars were still there if you wanted them, but so too was a new and revolutionary kind of book – one that ditched the traditional wordy approach in favour of linguistic short-cuts designed to take the hard slog out of language learning and to produce immediate results for the sound-bite generation.

Meanwhile, an altogether bigger revolution was underway. With the dissolution of the Soviet Union in 1991, the map of eastern Europe was redrawn. *Teach Yourself Romanian* (1992), *Teach Yourself Czech* (1993), *Teach Yourself Serbo-Croat* (1993) and similar books on the Slavonic languages had to tread a careful path through an ever-changing geopolitical landscape and wisely stuck to generalisations that would hold in the most likely of future scenarios. Even into the new millennium, the favoured policy was neutrality. Thus, *Teach Yourself Ukrainian* (2003) has the following introduction:

> Ukraine is one of the new countries on the map of Europe but the language and history of the people who live there can be traced back at least as far as the 10th century.

While *Teach Yourself Serbian* (2003) contains this:

> Serbia did not escape internal conflict when ethnic Albanians demanded greater autonomy for the southern province of Kosovo which has been administered by the UN since June 1999.

Closer to home, an updated *Teach Yourself Welsh* (2003) also takes in recent political developments and presents them in characteristically neutral terms:

> The creation of the National Assembly in 1999 and the development of Cardiff as an important administrative and cultural capital mean that Wales and the Welsh language can look forward with confidence to the future.

The new millennium saw a reinvigoration of the language series, with sumptuous colour photographs on the covers promising excitement, discovery and a world of new sensations:

> Welcome to a new experience. If you have never tried to learn a Chinese language before you are in for a rare treat.

So reads the introduction to *Teach Yourself Cantonese* (2003), which goes on encouragingly:

> They [the Chinese] love it when foreigners stammer out their first words of Cantonese because there is bound to be a howler or two which can be punned into something funny. Don't be put off, you are brightening their lives and they will not despise you for it.

Good to know that while they were chuckling at you and metaphorically whacking you about the head with a pig's bladder, they were, in fact, being immeasurably cheered up. And you, simultaneously, were performing the very important function of "brightening their lives".

Reassuring, that, and alone worth every penny of the cover price.

Teach Yourself Beginner's Japanese (2003) has similar words of encouragement from the off:

> Japanese is still regarded as an "exotic" language by many people and believed to be "too difficult to learn". Nothing could be further from the truth.

It adds, counter-intuitively for those who had taught themselves tantric sex in 2001:

> A little often is far more effective than a long session every now and then.

Sayonara. And now for something completely different. From the late 1990s, a new language series was introduced aimed not so much at replacing the traditional, grammar-based books as at complementing them with a radical new approach to language learning. The "Instant" series was born with its introduction of "good news grammar", which it breezily describes as follows:

> After you read it you can forget half of it and still succeed! That's why it's good news.

This may have been heresy to grammarians and linguistic purists, but the series editors were unmoved. *Teach Yourself Instant Italian* (2006), for example, "has been structured for your rapid success" and was designed to "cut frills and boredom and concentrate on the essentials". *Instant Spanish* (2006) went further, offering "no ghastly grammar – just a few useful tips and no time wasters such as 'the pen of my aunt'". There were to be no "phrase book phrases for taking up Flamenco in Bilbao" and everything was directed at learning to speak the language from day one.

Companion volumes followed suit, *Instant Japanese* (2006), for example, promises "no phrase book phrases for taking lessons in sumo wrestling", *Instant Russian* (2006), "no phrase book phrases for vodka sampling sessions in Siberia", and *Instant Portuguese* (2006), "no phrase book phrases for when you lose a crown from your front tooth while doing the city tour of Lisbon".

One imagines the author of *Teach Yourself to Learn a Foreign Language* (1965) to be spinning in his proverbial. Scourge of "Welsh in a Week" and "French in a Fortnight", he would surely have been offended by the premise of the initial undertaking: "No ghastly grammar – just a few useful tips!" and "After you read it you can forget half of it and still succeed!" But these were (and are) different times requiring different approaches. The series attracted a huge following and won plaudits, among others, from *The Independent* newspaper, which declared the books "A language lifeline; fun, fast, and easy." Plus ça change and all that.

CHAPTER VI

NEW WORLDS TO CONQUER

1970s

AND BEYOND

ALL KINDS OF EVERYTHING

Writing in his 1963 edition of *Teach Yourself Poetry*, Robin Skelton has this to say about his chosen subject:

This may seem an obvious point to make, but it is necessary to emphasize that poetry is always in a dynamic relationship with society. It does not exist to give readers what they are used to, but to show them that life is perpetually fascinating, wonderful, and new, and continually demands reappraisal.

The point could equally have been made about the Teach Yourself enterprise. It was never content to give us what we were used to but tried to introduce us to new possibilities. And, oh, what possibilities awaited us all on the threshold of a new decade! In the brave new world of 1969, Neil Armstrong and Buzz Aldrin became the first men to walk on the moon, "Monty Python's Flying Circus" was unveiled to a TV audience reared on Benny Hill, and Dana won the fifteenth Eurovision Song Contest with "All Kinds of Everything". It was an anthem that could have been written to herald in the 1970s, an era of promise and plenitude that began with the three-day week and ended in the winter of discontent.

Meanwhile, an ocean away from the creaky and crumbling facade of Britain's industrial relations, research and development was underway to produce a tiny component that would play its role in not only shaking up labour relations across the globe but in transforming the world of work for all time. In 1971, the microprocessor was unveiled and this unleashed the limitless potential of computer technology for all.

Teach Yourself was doing its bit to keep up to speed with fast-moving developments and was quick off the mark with *Teach Yourself Computer*

Programming (1970). However, *Teach Yourself Heraldry and Genealogy*, published in the same year, showed that there was room in the catalogue for both the ancient and the modern. As if to underline that very fact, the experts behind *Teach Yourself Shooting* (1970) deployed their expertise on a traditional pastime that transported all to an untroubled corner of the Hampshire countryside.

The joy of the shoot

Most of my longest and dearest friendships have risen from shooting encounters in England and abroad, and it has been my good fortune during my shooting life to witness some first class marksmanship with all types of fire-arm, watch with fascination displays of wood and fieldcraft by experts, and myself learn something of the wile and wariness of game of all species and sizes. I can only hope that every reader of this book will, in the days ahead, be able to cherish as many memories.

Teach Yourself Shooting, 1970

Despite the evolving style of the Teach Yourself books, the introduction, reprinted as late as 1976, is an endearing return to the house style of the 1940s and 1950s:

> Representing one of the world's leading gun-makers, it gives me the greatest pleasure to sponsor this book and welcome the reader into the shooting fraternity, a brotherhood without equal. I have been fortunate to have held a gun in my hand since my boyhood days and, albeit the years are now rolling by, I still look forward to my next day in the open air with just the same enthusiasm as in those halcyon days when my lungs did not protest at any exertion and my legs supported me without complaint over the roughest ground or steepest hill!

Duly welcomed into the shooting fraternity, the reader was then sent on his way with ceremony:

> It now only remains for me to wish every reader "good hunting", with the hope that the contents of this book will help him over the first few stepping stones of his shooting career.

The beginner was first introduced to the gun-dog which, if well-trained, "is often worth half a line of beaters." Useful on the field, the dog could also be a companionable presence in the home:

> A gun-dog can be not only a great asset to the novice sportsman but a delightful household pet as well, and no harm is done if it is

befriended perforce during the weekdays by a wife or any person with whom its owner is living, who can give it affection, regular exercise, and meals.

But, for goodness sake, don't confuse the little fellow:

Have an earnest talk with your wife, or whoever it may be, that the puppy is to answer to only one name and must not be called, say, "Rufus" by you and "Squiffles" by her.

Figure 20 *Teach Yourself Shooting,* 1970

We learn the value of good training – or rather, the dangers of insufficient training – several pages later when the author, Maurice Turner, takes us out onto the fields to bag the partridge. The mutt in question has bolted at the first sign of a hare and thereby set everything back by half an hour as the shooting party has lowered its guns:

Its owner smites his brow and declares that
this is the very first time such a thing has
happened. The dog is cautioned until its
owner's throat is sore.

There is worse to come and, with scarcely
concealed contempt, Maurice Turner spares us no
detail of the embarrassing spectacle before him:

A sign of complete lack of training reveals itself
when the dog rolls on its back and sticks its
paws in the air.

You see, call a dog Squiffles and this is what
happens. It would never have happened with Rufus.

THE OFFICE

The importance of proper training in every sphere
of activity could never be stressed enough, as
Josephine Shaw informed us in *Teach Yourself
Office Practice* (1972). With the no-nonsense
manner of a hospital matron from the Hattie
Jacques school, she begins as she means to go on:

If office procedures are to be carried out
effectively and your work is to be done in the
minimum time compatible with efficiency, it is
essential to work to a plan – by the day, by the
week and by the month.

And go on she does, from essential office
equipment to the all-important matters of dress
and grooming:

> Clothes need not be "sensible" to be suitable
> for the office, but they should not be extreme.

So loon pants were right out. In fact, Figure 21
gives you a glimpse of the ideals – a high-necked
sailor-suit blouse worn by the Farrah Fawcett look-
alike standing by the "Twinlock visible card index".

Figure 21 *Teach Yourself Office Practice*, 1972

The telephone manner was a crucial skill to master
since the telephone, "provided that it is used properly,
can be your firm's greatest asset" and was "the most
important piece of machinery in any office".

Secretaries were told never to sound in a hurry, to
put a smile in their voices, and always to stick to
the correct form of words in preference to slang. A
checklist is helpfully provided:

Slang	**Correct Expression**
Hello (when answering a call).	Good morning (followed by name of department or individual).
OK; alright.	Yes, certainly.
Will do.	I shall do that.
Hold on.	Will you hold the line, please?
He's not in; he's out.	I'm sorry Mr Jones is not in. Can I help you?
'bye.	Goodbye.
He's busy.	I'm sorry, Mr Jones is not available at present. May I ask him to ring you later?

At the distance of only thirty years, the sheer cumbersome bulk of the office equipment is immediately striking. The Gestetner offset duplicator looks like an iron-lung, the telephones look like cement lumps, and the telex machine has the proportions of a small-scale Wurlitzer. The reader is, however, guided reassuringly around this Flintstone-esque office landscape and along the way given tips on everything from welcoming a visitor to preparing a good business letter. In short, it is "ideal for all secretaries, clerical workers and personal assistants".

The book has the back-to-the-future feel of BBC's "Tomorrow's World" in its 1970s heyday, when the programme showcased the latest technological gadgetry and regularly attracted ten

million viewers per show. This was the era, you may
remember, of such marvels as the pocket calculator,
the digital watch, and Teletext, upon which we
gazed like woodland Hobbits staring at glass beads.

GETTING ON

For all the get-up-and-go types equipping
themselves with the new technological wonders of
the 1970s and forging ahead in their state-of-the-art
offices, there were a few sad individuals destined
never to make it. Their unfulfilled lives were
presented to readers as cautionary tales, to show
us how we would end up if we lacked the
necessary drive or focus. We were introduced to
one instructive case in *Teach Yourself
Salesmanship* (1972):

> On one occasion, when passing through a
> department of a great London shop, the
> general manager nodded pleasantly to a
> middle-aged salesman standing behind the
> counter and said to the friend accompanying
> him: "That chap and I started as apprentices
> together thirty-five years ago."
>
> "Why is he still behind the counter?"
>
> "In our early days together he never seemed to
> have any plan to his life; he didn't seem to
> know where he was going or how to get there."
>
> "Kind of aiming at nothing and hitting it, eh?"
>
> "Yes, I suppose that's about it."

Yet with the right attitude and, of course, an appropriate book to study (his own), S. A. Williams encourages the potential salesman to be a success in life. A mixture of psychology, soft soap and the hard sell, the book fine-tunes the art of salesmanship by taking the beginner through the opening moves of a sale, the mid-phase and the closure, all the while stressing the importance of good, clear English. The tone of the book suggests a rigid hierarchy of sales personnel and managers and hints at a British class system as firmly in place in 1972 as it had been in the 1950s. It could easily have been the template – minus the jokes – for the BBC comedy programme "Are You Being Served?" which was first aired that same year.

Minding your language

Gross errors in grammar, serious mistakes of pronunciation, and the obvious misuse of words tend to create a feeling of superiority over the person who makes them which is most damaging to the right relations between customer and salesman. This does not mean that the salesman should try to cultivate a mode of speech or accent foreign to that which is native to him. His customers would naturally regard this as an affectation, and would either ridicule it or resent it as a form of "swank".

Teach Yourself Salesmanship, 1972

TIME OFF

Outside the shop and the office, Teach Yourself was busy catering for our leisure hours. Peter Turner's *Teach Yourself Introducing Hi-Fi* (1976) was, in many ways, a classic of the time. Packed with the technological specifications of this or that amplifier or speaker, it also acted as a user-friendly guide to a plethora of products that were becoming affordable to an increasingly large group of non-specialist consumers. Turner's opening CV-cum-blurb conjures up a man constantly moving with the times – a geek for all seasons to some, but to others an endearing mix of the contemporary and the traditional:

> Peter Turner first began listening to reproduced music on an Edison-cylinder machine belonging to a friend's father, and vividly recalls the days of the crystal-set and the moving-iron loudspeaker. From these beginnings he has developed a life-long interest in both music and hi-fi, and in recent years, tape recording. He is a passionate believer that technique is the servant of the art, seeing hi-fi as a means to an end, but as the means which must be understood in order to attain the end.

It was a timely book, and one that would soon be updated to encompass the personal stereo and the compact disc. For an idea of just how much else was waiting around the corner you needed only to have asked two fellow geeks, Steve Jobs and Steve

Wozniak, who got together to form the Apple Computer Company that same year. Or you might have phoned one Bill Gates who was busy registering his new company's trade name, "Microsoft".

If the pace of technological change in the 1970s was leaving you breathless, you could always reach for something more traditional and distinctly low-tech: *Teach Yourself Growing Orchids in the Home* (1975) or *Teach Yourself Candlemaking* (1976) perhaps.

With or without *Teach Yourself the Darts Player's Handbook* (1979), Margaret Thatcher hit the bullseye that year by becoming the first woman prime minister of the UK and ushering in eighteen years of Conservative Party rule. The period is recalled almost thirty years later by Logan Murray whose *Teach Yourself Stand-Up Comedy* (2007) summarises it (not exactly objectively) as a time when:

> Clause 28 was trying to push gay people back into the closet. The 'sus' laws gave carte blanche [sic] to black men being stopped and searched for no good reason. Whole communities were being uprooted through deregulation and sell-offs; instead of sympathy and protection people were told to "get on your bike" and look for work – any work – even if it meant the break up of the family. Sleaze and corruption abounded, brown paper envelopes stuffed with notes were finding their way into the back pockets of MPs. Here at last was a

really objectionable political party for critical
comedians to get their teeth into.

Come on, Logan, don't sit on the fence. Tell us
what you really think, man. And will you be voting
Tory next time?

Teach Yourself Amateur Theatre (1980) kicked
off the Thatcher decade with a wistful backwards
glance at an earlier epoch when the club and the
society were considered the natural by-products of
a thriving cultural life. The amateur dramatic
society was such a group of like-minded
enthusiasts. Ideally, it was a *company* united by a
common sense of purpose and it was supportive of
each other's disparate talents – not a self-serving
clique of neurotic back-stabbers and prima donnas
prepared to auction their grannies for the lead in
Salad Days. The author Jennifer Curry puts it
more tactfully:

> I feel very strongly that full membership of an
> amateur dramatic society should only be
> granted to those who are prepared to do some
> other job than acting, when called upon, and
> that this should be clearly stated on the
> membership application form they sign when
> they join.

Her approach to the all-important choice of play
was wide ranging and inclusive but also cautious
and realistic:

> If you want to give them Pinter, condition them
> first with *The Caretaker* before tackling the

lesser known, less universally entertaining ones. Samuel Beckett should be discreetly infiltrated into your list with *Waiting for Godot*, which is "effective theatre" for most people, if not wholly understood.

However, audience reaction alone was not the deciding factor. You had to consider the company, too:

> I have seen good, lively societies grind to a halt because the committee has decided that they should stage a succession of music-halls, pantomimes and revues when what the actors wanted to do was Sartre, Pinter and Beckett. It must be equally galling for a group set upon recreating *Salad Days* or the *Dancing Years* to find themselves struggling through *Mahagonny* ... In other words, by all means let the company have a go at *King Lear* if they are good enough and the prospect excites them, but follow it up with *Move Over Mrs Markham* or *Charley's Aunt*. A mixed diet of theatre is essential.

Indeed the "mixed diet" approach was a core principle of the entire series. Throughout the 1970s and early 1980s, a sub-series under the general heading of "Care and Welfare" was published with such titles as *Depression*, *One-Parent Families*, *Schizophrenia*, *Understanding Child Abuse* and *Drugs in Perspective*. These co-existed quite happily with volumes like *Teach Yourself Lawns* (1979) ("The British home lawn is the envy of the world") and *Teach Yourself*

Growing Vegetables (1978) in the equally popular "World of the Garden" series. The more the series changed, the more it stayed the same – providing authoritative information on the widest possible range of pursuits and always being relevant to the changing needs of successive generations.

NOUVELLE CUISINE

Teach Yourself Vegetable Cookery (1980) was a direct descendant of its 1938 counterpart *Teach Yourself to Cook*, but it was updated to suit an age that had grown more specialised and discerning in its tastes and that now had the opportunity to grow vegetable varieties largely unheard of seventy years previously. In fact, some extracts recall the style of the earlier book. "Adventuring" in cookery had been promoted by Evelyn White in 1938; Frances Naldrett seems to be advocating it again in the 1980s:

> Vegetables ... are versatile ... and can be served alone or combined with other ingredients, raw or cooked, with a sauce or plain. Apart from their role as an accompaniment to meat and fish, vegetables can make a main meal in their own right. With the addition of nuts, a little cheese, eggs or small quantities of meat and fish they provide all the nourishment we need.

Thrift, too, was one of the qualities Naldrett encouraged. If growing your own from a grow-bag on the patio was stage one, stage two involved coping with a mega crop without wasting a bean:

> Most fresh, young and tender vegetables need
> no more than a knob of butter and a sprinkling
> of salt and pepper added after cooking but if
> there is a glut or when the vegetables get older,
> a more sophisticated treatment can turn them
> into a totally different dish.

Cleverly, the book did not limit itself to "vegetarian" recipes, and its basic soup stock incorporated "mixed bones, bacon rinds and meat trimmings". As a result, it widened its appeal to the non-vegetarian and the out-and-out carnivore.

Teach Yourself Home Preserving (1980) was another variation on the standard theme of cooking but it went well beyond mere jam and chutney making. This was serious stuff and its author, Judy Ridgway, provided complete instructions for potting meat, salting and smoking fish, and even storing root vegetables outdoors in a clamp. And it even had a glancing reference to that constant if invisible benchmark of human progress – early man:

> Some methods of home preserving have been
> in use for thousands of years. Drying, salting
> and smoking, for example, were almost
> certainly used by the very early civilisations to
> preserve summer produce for long winter
> months.

Nevertheless, humanity's progress was patchy. At least if the introduction to *Teach Yourself Public Speaking* (1980) was to be believed:

> While, in general, the standards of the mass-produced things of life have sunk lamentably low, the standards of individual expertise, from brain surgery to running a mile, have grown better and better – and this certainly applies to public speaking.

Even in 1980 there was a rather old-fashioned ring to the text with the author advising, for example, that tissues should be carried at all times en route to speaking engagements:

> These can act as substitute towels, shoe and spectacle cleaners, handkerchiefs, napkins, wiping the train's dirty windows for a view of the scenery, cleaning buffet car cutlery and a host of other little jobs which make for hygiene and travelling comfort.

The following year delivered a shock to this ordered view of the world when large-scale rioting in Brixton, South London wrecked many shops and left hundreds injured. Still, later that year the Charles and Diana wedding put a smile back on everyone's face as the country turned out at street parties to celebrate. Judy Ridgway was again on hand to provide the appropriately festive food with her *Teach Yourself Mixer, Blender and Processor Cookery* (1981), building on the growing popularity of labour-saving gadgets in the home and kitchen. She was less evangelical than Caroline Haslett before her (she of the Electrical Association for Women), but was still capable of transports of enthusiasm over ham and tongue mousses, savoury catherine wheels, and kipper soufflés. And, above all, she was a great encourager:

> All the recipes in the book have been tested on friends and relatives who, in many cases, have been inspired to get out appliances which have been tucked away in inaccessible cupboards unused for some time. I sincerely hope that they will do the same for all my readers.

ROLAND RAT AND THE POST-INDUSTRIAL AGE

By the 1980s, with fifty years behind it, it seemed that there was nothing the Teach Yourself series could not tackle. *Teach Yourself Who's Who in the Old Testament* (1982) appeared in the same year that *Teach Yourself Weather Forecasting for Sailors* burst on the scene and Argentina invaded the Falklands. When Britons were not following the progress of the British Task Force to the South Atlantic, they could relax with a choice of *Teach Yourself Card Games for all the Family*, *Teach Yourself Company Law*, *Teach Yourself Alcoholism*, *Teach Yourself Family Law* or *Teach Yourself Conservation*.

At the end of 1982, *Time Magazine* set a precedent by awarding its title "Man of the Year" not to a person but to a thing: the personal computer. Coincidentally or otherwise, in 1983 Teach Yourself launched the first of a raft of titles devoted to computer programming in FORTRAN, Pascal and MSX basic, and a year later, *Teach Yourself Computers and their Use* (1984).

This was the decade of the Yuppy (young urban professional) and the new Romantics, of Breakfast TV and Roland Rat, of *Flashdance* legwarmers and the Rubik's Cube, the decade when the industrial age finally handed over the torch to the information age. In 1984, the first home Macintosh computer appeared and, although that fateful year had been used by George Orwell as shorthand for the dystopian nightmare that awaited us all, the most we had to fear was a weekly dose of "Dallas" and "Dynasty" and the inexplicable popularity of the mullet hair-do.

By 1985, with the implications of computer technology becoming ever clearer, the Teach Yourself editors felt that introducing microcomputers in business would be a good idea. So they did – with the aptly named *Teach Yourself Introducing Microcomputers in Business*. That year, the comedian Ernie Wise made the first British mobile phone call, "EastEnders" first aired on British TV, and the first Blockbuster Video Store opened in Dallas, Texas. However, even in the face of such modernity, the standard Teach Yourself texts, duly updated or revised, kept appearing on a backlist that looked as solid and reassuring as ever – *Teach Yourself Bee-keeping* (1986), *Teach Yourself Latin* (1986) *Teach Yourself Golf* (1988) and *Teach Yourself Welding* (1989).

The decline of traditional manufacturing industry had a big impact on people's working lives and, as the 1990s wore on, Teach Yourself became ever more attuned to the corporate world, producing training books for all levels of workers and managers and helping them to progress smoothly up the business ladder. *Teach Yourself Winning at Job Interviews* (1994) began with stage one: getting a job in the first place. Dealing with the demands of group interviews, panel interviews and lunch interviews ("stay away from alcohol, choose a meal that is easy to eat, not messy, do not talk too much") were among the thousands of tips the author disclosed. He stressed the importance of preparation before the interview, the importance of presentation during the interview, and the importance of follow-up afterwards (a short letter of thanks and a thorough self-analysis). In his list of preconceptions and stereotypes that "can work for you or against you" he details the following:

- Tall and skinny people are nervous and impatient.
- Fat people are lazy.
- People who don't drink are a bit strange.
- Women are too emotional and therefore unpredictable.
- People with beards are introverts and misfits.
- Unemployed people would accept any job.
- People with accents cannot be trusted.

He admitted these perceptions were irrational and unfair – but also that there was nothing much you could do about most of them. Even Teach Yourself had its limitations.

In 1997, Mrs Thatcher's successor John Major handed over political power to Anthony Charles Lynton Blair, who unveiled the New Labour project and became the youngest UK prime minister in 185 years. As if to match those heady high spirits – or just possibly by pure coincidence – a celebratory *Teach Yourself Line Dancing* appeared in 1998:

> Welcome, Friend. You have taken your first courageous step towards becoming a line-dancer. Be warned, once you have mastered the dances and started to mix with other line dancers, once you have experienced the warm, friendly atmosphere and moved to the rhythmic strains of a live country and western band, you're hooked. This book could possibly change your whole way of life.

Extravagant praise for the dance of our times

Line dance fever! Can there be anyone on this planet who has not heard or seen line dancing? I think not. It is certainly experiencing a popularity explosion.
        Teach Yourself Line Dancing, 1998

Able to adapt itself to the pro-market Blairite agenda, Teach Yourself continued to publish guides for the changing workplace. *Teach Yourself Winning in the Job Market* (1998), written by a seasoned recruitment specialist, took the search for employment to the next level. Its aim was for would-be hot shots to improve their marketability and plan their short-, medium- and long-term career strategies. It was not enough, the author claimed, to wing it. Preparation and a realistic appraisal of skills were vital for landing the right job. Why? Because:

> Behind the smart offices and the neat industrial parks that are a feature of today's industrial and commercial scene is one single, simple fact; today's jobs market is a jungle.

MAKE LOVE NOT WAR

Teach Yourself seemed well aware of the highly competitive nature of the late twentieth-century workplace, and as the third millennium dawned, it produced a number of titles like *Teach Yourself Surviving Your Organization* (2001) and *Teach Yourself Teams and Team Working* (2002), dealing with the mechanics of companies and corporations. It also took note of the dotcom bubble and encouraged people to set up their own small businesses.

For budding Richard Bransons and Alan Sugars, *Teach Yourself Entrepreneurship* (2006) is the book to read. The title contains exhaustive information on building up, sustaining and expanding a successful business. "So, 912 out of 1,000 people would sooner be running their own business than being an employee", it begins. "I dedicate this book to those 912."

Ten questions that get you focused

1. *What would make me happiest if I achieved it today?*
2. *Who would benefit most by what I offer?*
3. *Where are the quickest results to be found?*
4. *What is the most valuable thing I could do right now?*
5. *What action should I take now?*
6. *What question would I like to know the answer to?*
7. *Who am I letting down by not calling them now?*
8. *What or who is closest to making me money?*
9. *What are my priorities?*
10. *Can I spend more time with prospects offering higher returns?*

Teach Yourself Entrepreneurship, 2006

Yet those individuals carving out businesses for themselves are doing so in an increasingly globalised world. Broadband internet, the information superhighway, developments in transport and electronic communications, the primacy of multinationals, transnationals and megacorporations have gradually been making the world both smaller and more homogenised. While many of the Teach Yourself titles reflect this, they also give space to the spiritual backlash. In 1977, *Teach Yourself Meditation* put its finger on the problem:

> Who can fail to recognise the spiritual vacuum in our midst? Orthodox religion is fast losing its hold.

As a result, there is no shortage of Teach Yourself books on exotic belief systems and alternative therapies, including crystal healing, reiki, Ayurveda, Feng Shui, hand reflexology, aromatherapy, Indian head massage, and Tai Chi.

If this plethora of therapies fails to bring you peace of mind, you could always turn to *Teach Yourself How to Win at Horse Racing* (2003), which promises a life of financial bliss beyond your wildest dreams. Anyone familiar with a high-street betting office will also know its atmosphere of pure nicotine and heroic despair. The book is the antithesis of this and brings an element of the scientific into the picture. Indeed, it gives every impression, at least to the casual reader, of having more in common with *Teach Yourself Arithmetic* with its focus on odds, probability, and the maximisation of returns. However, it isn't above a little native cunning when advising how to winkle out of bookmakers information they would rather keep close to their chest:

Betting shops keep their limits for large bets confidential, but it is fairly easy to discover them with a little stealth. Simply write out a large bet on a horse that has the same price as the one you want to bet on. Hand it to the cashier and pretend to be looking for your wallet. If the bet is passed to the manager and he reaches for the phone, you know you have exceeded the limit. If nothing happens, you know you can safely bet on your selection. Whatever the outcome, ask for the slip to be returned as you cannot find your wallet. You can then write out a slip for your selection, safe in the knowledge that you will not be offered a reduced price.

To increase your chances of attaining financial Nirvana, you could also dip into *How to Win at Poker* (2003) and *How to Win at Online Gambling* (2006). Better still, try *Teach Yourself Astrology* (2007) to discover whether a windfall really is written in the stars. If it isn't and you went ahead anyway, losing your shirt on the cards or the horses, *Teach Yourself Counselling* (2007) is on hand – or even *Teach Yourself Managing Stress* (2007) and *Teach Yourself Happiness* (2007).

Those looking to achieve fame and fortune by more conventional means could find inspiration from *Teach Yourself How to Write a Blockbuster* (2006), which is a practical guide to nurturing, honing and ultimately marketing natural literary talent. Writing a book, however, is the final step in the process. Before that is the small matter of ideas followed, crucially, by the everyday observation needed to flesh out those ideas and create credible characters:

> Writers tend to be avid people-watchers, endlessly fascinated by the things people do or say, and it's this constant study of other people that gives their characters depth and truth. So make people-watching your hobby. Observe the parade of humanity around you, and write down the tics and traits that catch your attention: the seventeen year old girl who sucks her thumb when she thinks no one is looking; the man in the smart suit who squints his eyes almost shut as he reads.

If that sounds familiar, it is. Compare it with *Teach Yourself to Write* (1942), and you will see that not much has changed. Having said that, perhaps few in 1942 would have foreseen that, sixty years later, *Writing Erotic Fiction* (1997) would make it to the catalogue, raising no more eyebrows than *Teach Yourself Quilting* (2000).

It is probably true that the founding father of the series, the conservative and devoutly religious Leonard Cutts, would have had a moment's demur before commissioning *Teach Yourself Flirting*, *Teach Yourself Great Sex* or *Teach Yourself Tantric Sex*, but that is hardly surprising. He was very much the product of his times and times have changed. An educated man who certainly would have known a lingam from a yoni when he saw one, Cutts himself would have accepted that the days when sex manuals were stored away on "high furniture" (*Teach Yourself Sex; Its Meaning and Purpose*, 1951) were long gone and that somehow the series would have to adapt to survive. However, what he would have made of *Teach Yourself the Kama Sutra* (2007) is probably best left to the imagination:

> For Kama Sutra-style sex, here are some traditional and modern clothing ideas for women (who are otherwise naked apart from jewellery). Wear:
>
> - a short bolero
> - a wide belt
> - a choker and elbow-length gloves
> - suspender belt and a pair of boots
> - suspender belt with fishnet stockings and a half cup bra

And just as you can bear the excitement no longer:

> - a cowboy hat (and chaps if you can get them).

Men are also given some style tips for the night of passion:

> Men: wear clothes that emphasise the power of your shoulders. Maybe grow a moustache – a sign of virility to the Hindus. Work out at the gym to develop your muscles.

And, "naked apart from jewellery", he should wear:

- a bandana, scarf, or hat
- a waistcoat (optional)
- a tie (optional).

Hard to believe that this Burt Reynolds school of horizontal jogging was written in 2007, but it was – with due deference to the ancient erotic master, Vatsayayana. The author persuades readers to overcome their inhibitions and concedes that "you might feel rather silly at first using Vatsayayana's techniques". Though probably not half as silly as standing there stark naked sporting a tash and chaps.

What would Leonard Cutts have made of it all? At least he could have concluded, along with *The News of the World*, that "all human life is there". Not a bad legacy really. If he were to look at today's catalogue and a backlist that includes such apparently lightweight titles as *Teach Yourself Decluttering* alongside the more heavyweight *Teach Yourself Stalin's Russia*, he might also conclude that the series is still in safe hands. We are, after all, in a post-modern world in which John Keats and Bob Dylan are co-equals. So why shouldn't books on caravanning and baby massage hold their own against those on the Cold War and astronomy? "No reason whatsoever, old boy," Cutts might say, "I could have told you that seventy years ago. Now what about an early lunch?"

GIVE INSTRUCTION
TO A WISE MAN . . .